VEGETARIAN **MEDITERRANEAN**-STYLE

VEGETARIAN
MEDITERRANEAN-
STYLE

ACADEMIA
BARILLA

The Taunton Press

Original edition © 2015 by De Agostini Libri S.p.A.

The Taunton Press
Inspiration for hands-on living®

The Taunton Press, Inc.
63 South Main Street
PO Box 5506, Newtown, CT 06470-5506
e-mail: tp@taunton.com

Translations:

Irina Oryshkevich - Catherine Howard - Rosetta Translations SARL - Mary Doyle -
John Venerella - Free z'be, Paris - Salvatore Ciolfi - Contextus s.r.l., Pavia - Helen Farrell

LIBRARY OF CONGRESS CATALOGING-IN-PUBLICATION DATA IN PROGRESS

ISBN: 978-1-62710-768-6

Printed in China

10 9 8 7 6 5 4 3 2 1

EDITED BY

ACADEMIA BARILLA

INTRODUCTION

GIANLUIGI ZENTI

TEXT

LORENA CARRARA
CHEF MARIO GRAZIA
MARIAGRAZIA VILLA

RECIPES

CHEF MARIO GRAZIA

PHOTOGRAPHS

CHEF MARIO GRAZIA
CHEF STEFANO LODI
CHEF MATTEO MANFERDINI
CHATO MORANDI
ALBERTO ROSSI
LUCIO ROSSI
CHEF LUCA ZANGA

ACADEMIA BARILLA EDITORIAL COORDINATION

CHATO MORANDI
LEANNE KOSINSKI
ILARIA ROSSI

GRAPHIC DESIGN

PAOLA PIACCO

CONTENTS

LIST OF RECIPES

THE MEDITERRANEAN STYLE

Good news! You can choose among foods that are sustainable, healthful and light without sacrificing the pleasure of Italian cuisine. Italy has countless luminaries inspired by a "green" way of life and its gastronomic culture has consistently been full of delicious vegetarian dishes.

A diet that excludes meat and fish is a well-established way of life for people around the world. In Italy alone, those who professed to be vegetarian (the term derives from the Latin adjective vegetus, meaning healthy) are legion: from Pythagoras, with his celebrated "Pythagorean Diet," deriving from the belief in the transmigration of souls, to Empedocles of Agrigento, who preached abstinence from eating animals of the earth and sea; from the philosopher Seneca to the poet Ovid; from Tertullian, the writer, to Porphyry of Tyre, the philosopher. Although during the Middle Ages it was primarily the members of monastic orders who practiced a strict vegetarian diet, in the Renaissance, there were also artists who did so, the most prominent of whom was Leonardo da Vinci.

For a person who wants to become a vegetarian, there is no need to look exclusively to the tables of the East, where many people traditionally follow a diet excluding meat or fish for religious reasons. We can observe Italian recipes dating back to ancient times that were often

PREPARED WITH NEITHER MEAT NOR FISH. IN MANY CASES, THESE PREPARATIONS EPITOMIZE THE VARIOUS REGIONAL CUISINES AND REFLECT THE VERY ESSENCE OF THE SO-CALLED MEDITERRANEAN DIET. FOR EXAMPLE, TWO NATIONAL STARS, SPAGHETTI WITH TOMATO SAUCE AND PIZZA MARGHERITA, ARE PURELY VEGETARIAN.

COMPARED WITH SOME OTHER "GREEN-FOOD" PHILOSOPHIES, THAT OF ITALIAN CUISINE IS RICH IN FLAVOR WITHOUT ELABORATE PREPARATIONS OR ABUNDANT SPICES. THE KEY IS THAT ITALIAN DISHES USE REGIONAL INGREDIENTS OF THE HIGHEST QUALITY AND MOST DYNAMIC FLAVORS IN WAYS THAT BRING OUT THE BEST IN THEM. DEEP WITHIN ITS SOUL, TRADITIONAL ITALIAN FOOD IS ALREADY CHARACTERIZED AS LACTO-OVO-VEGETARIAN. AND WHILE IT IS AN OLD SOUL, IT HAS MODERN POTENTIAL TO GROW. IT IS ESTIMATED THAT THE NUMBER OF PEOPLE TURNING TO A DIET FREE FROM ANIMAL PRODUCTS WILL INCREASE NOTICEABLY IN THE COMING YEARS, WHETHER FOR HEALTH, HUMANITARIAN OR ECOLOGIC REASONS. ITALIAN CUISINE, ALREADY ONE OF THE MOST BELOVED IN THE WORLD, MAY BECOME EVEN MORE SO, OWING TO ITS "HEART OF GREEN."

ACADEMIA BARILLA, AN INTERNATIONAL CENTER DEDICATED TO THE PROMOTION OF ITALIAN CUISINE, HAS COLLECTED A SELECTION OF VEGETARIAN RECIPES FOR THIS VOLUME: MOST ORIGINATE IN THE VAST HERITAGE OF REGIONAL CUISINES, SOME ARE ITALIAN BECAUSE OF THEIR USE OF STELLAR LOCAL PRODUCTS, OTHERS ARE RENOWNED FOR THEIR PURE CREATIVITY. WITH THESE DISHES VEGETARIAN LIFE BECOMES VERY ALLURING INDEED.

STARTERS

CHAPTER ONE

TOMATO AND BASIL BRUSCHETTA

BRUSCHETTA CON OLIO

Preparation time: 20 minutes + 2 hours and 5 minutes cooking time

4 Servings

1 baguette
1 clove garlic, peeled
11 oz. (300 g) canned tomatoes, diced
1 tbsp. plus 1 tsp. (20 ml) extra-virgin
   olive oil
4 fresh basil leaves, thinly sliced
Salt to taste

Method

Slice the baguette into pieces about 1/2 inch (1 cm) thick and toast them in the oven under the broiler for about 2 minutes on each side or in a dry skillet set over medium heat.

Lightly rub the garlic over the toasted bread.

Place the tomatoes in a bowl, and season them with the oil, basil, and salt. Let the tomato mixture sit for a few minutes to allow the flavors to blend.

Spread the tomato mixture evenly over the slices of toast and serve.

Difficulty

ROMAN JEWISH-STYLE ARTICHOKES

CARCIOFI ALLA GIUDIA

Preparation time: 20 minutes + 25 minutes cooking time

4 Servings

4 globe artichokes
Juice of 1 **lemon**
Extra-virgin olive oil, for frying
Salt and freshly ground black pepper
   to taste

Method

Remove the hard outer leaves of the artichokes until you reach the tender pale green or yellow leaves and cut the stems, leaving about 1 inch (3 cm) below the base of the artichoke. With a very sharp knife, cut off the top third of the leaves. Immediately put the trimmed artichokes in a bowl of water with lemon juice so they do not discolor.

Meanwhile, heat about 2 to 3 inches of oil (enough to almost cover the artichokes) in a deep skillet to 270°F (130°C) on a candy or deep-fry thermometer.

Drain the artichokes and pat them dry with a kitchen towel. Flatten them gently on a chopping board and gently spread the leaves. Sprinkle salt and pepper inside the leaves.

Fry the artichokes, turning occasionally with tongs, for about 20 minutes, or until a knife can easily pierce the flesh. Transfer to paper towels, stem side up to drain well. (This step can be completed up to 3 hours ahead; remove the oil from the heat, cover, and reserve.)

Just before serving the artichokes, reheat the oil to 350°F (175°C) and fry the artichokes head down for 3 to 5 minutes, until they are crunchy. Transfer them to clean paper towels to drain, then serve hot with a sprinkle of salt.

Difficulty

FRIED ZUCCHINI BLOSSOMS
FIORI DI ZUCCA FRITTI

15 minutes + 10 minutes cooking time

6 Servings

7 oz. (200 g) **all-purpose flour**
1 **large egg**
1/2 cup (100 ml) **water**
15 **zucchini blossoms**
Vegetable oil, for frying
Salt

Method

In a bowl, mix the flour with the egg and the water, stirring until the batter reaches the right texture (when dipped in it, the flower should be covered in a thin coating).

Wash the blossoms, then gently dry them. Remove and discard the pistils. Heat 1 inch of oil in a deep skillet to 350°F (175°C) on a candy or deep-fry thermometer. In batches of 5, dip the blossoms in the batter, coating them completely and letting excess batter drip off. Fry the coated blossoms in the oil, turning with a slotted spoon until nicely golden, 2 to 3 minutes. Transfer to paper towels to drain. Sprinkle with salt and serve immediately.

Difficulty

Did you know that...

Fried zucchini blossoms can be enjoyed as a unique and delicious dessert. Instead of seasoning the warm fried blossoms with salt, dust them with confectioners' sugar.

EGGPLANT ROLLS WITH GOAT CHEESE

INVOLTINI DI MELANZANE AL CAPRINO

Preparation time: 35 minutes + 10 minutes cooking time

4 Servings

1 3/4 lbs. (800 g) **eggplant (about 2 medium)**
Salt and freshly ground black pepper to taste
2/3 cup (150 ml) **extra-virgin olive oil**
10 1/2 oz. (300 g) **soft goat cheese**
1 **bunch fresh chives, thinly sliced**
14 oz. (400 g) **tomatoes (about 2 large), skinned and coarsely chopped**
12 oz. (350 g) **red onion (about 2 small), thinly sliced**
1 cup (250 ml) **white-wine vinegar**
2 tbsp. plus 2 tsp. (30 g) **sugar**
6 **large fresh basil leaves**

Method

Trim the eggplant, then cut them lengthwise into 1/4-inch-thick slices. Place the slices on a double thickness of paper towels, then salt generously and let them stand for 20 minutes. Pat dry with paper towels.

Heat 6 tablespoons oil in a nonstick pan over medium heat and cook the eggplant until tender and browned on both sides. When done, lay the eggplant on paper towels to absorb the excess oil.

Mix the goat cheese with the chives and season with salt and pepper to taste. In a food processor, purée the tomatoes with 2 tablespoons of olive oil. Strain the purée through a medium-mesh strainer and season with salt and pepper.

Heat the onions them in a pan with the vinegar and sugar. When the liquid reaches a boil, turn off the heat and strain it. Purée the basil with the remaining 2 tablespoons of olive oil.

Place a tablespoon of cheese in the middle of each eggplant slice and roll it up. Arrange the rolls, seam sides down, on serving plates with a spoonful of the sweet and sour onions, a spoonful of tomato purée, and a drizzle of basil oil.

Difficulty

Cook's Tip

For presentation and to help hold the rolls together, tie a length of fresh chive loosely around the rolls before serving.

BREADSTICKS IN THREE FLAVORS

GRISSINI ALL'OLIO EXTRA-VERGINE DI OLIVA AI TRE SAPORI

Preparation time: 20 minutes + 1 hour to rise + 15 minutes cooking time

4 Servings

1 tbsp. plus 1 1/2 tsp. (30 g) **active dry yeast**

1 cup (250 ml) **warm water (about 105°F / 40°C)**

4 cups (500 g) **Italian type "00" or all-purpose flour**

3 tbsp. plus 2 tsp. (50 ml) **extra-virgin olive oil**

1 3/4 tsp. (7 g) **sugar**

1 1/2 tsp. (10 g) **salt**

1 oz. (about 1 cup; 30 g) **fresh rosemary, leaves finely chopped**

3 tbsp. (20 g) **finely chopped sun-dried tomatoes**

3/4 oz. (20 g) **black olives, pitted and finely chopped**

Cornmeal for sprinkling

Method

Dissolve the yeast in 2/3 cup (150 ml) of the water. Combine with the flour, remaining water, oil, and sugar. Dissolve the salt in a few drops of water and add it at the very end. Divide the dough into 3 equal pieces. Mix the rosemary into 1 piece, the sun-dried tomatoes into another, and the olives into the third. Transfer each dough piece to a lightly oiled bowl and turn to coat. Cover the bowls with plastic wrap and let the doughs rise in a warm place until doubled in bulk, about 1 hour.

Heat the oven to 400°F (204°C).

Meanwhile, punch down 1 dough and turn it out onto a work surface. Cut the dough into 20 equal pieces and roll each into a 15- to 16-inch (40 cm) rope. Arrange the ropes 1 inch (3 cm) apart on 2 greased baking sheets sprinkled with cornmeal and let stand, uncovered, 15 minutes.

Bake the breadsticks in batches in the upper and lower thirds of the oven, switching the position of sheets halfway through baking, until golden-brown, 10 to 15 minutes. Transfer to racks to cool.

Difficulty

The origin of breadsticks

Although legend has it that the invention of breadsticks is linked to 17th-century history of the House of Savoy, it's more likely that breadsticks, or grissini, are simply an extreme version of gherrsa or grissia, a traditional Piedmontese bread, similar to the baguette that's still so popular in France. One thing is definite – breadsticks were long reserved for aristocratic tables only.

VEGETABLE CAPONATA
CAPONATA DI VERDURE

Preparation time: 30 minutes + 15 minutes cooking time

4 Servings

1 medium eggplant, diced
Salt and freshly ground black pepper
1/2 oz. (15 g) raisins (about
   1 1/2 tbsp.)
1/2 cup (100 ml) extra-virgin olive oil
2 oz. (50 g) onion (about 1 small),
   finely diced
2 oz. (50 g) celery (about 2 stalks),
   finely diced
3 1/2 oz. (100 g) zucchini (about
   1/2 medium), diced
1 oz. (20 g) salt-packed capers, rinsed
   and drained
2 tbsp. (15 g) pine nuts
1 oz. (25 g) black olives
3 1/2 oz. (100 g) crushed tomatoes
1 tsp. (5 ml) wine vinegar
1 tbsp. (10 g) sugar
2 tbsp. (15 g) chopped shelled
   unsalted pistachios
1 bunch fresh basil leaves, torn

Method

Put the diced eggplant in a colander, salt it lightly, and allow it to drain for about 30 minutes.

Soak the raisins in lukewarm water for 15 minutes. Drain the raisins and squeeze them to remove excess water.

Heat 1/3 cup of the oil in a large skillet over medium heat and fry the eggplant until lightly golden and tender. With a slotted spoon, transfer the eggplant to paper towels to drain.

Add the remainder of the oil to the skillet and heat over medium. Sauté the onion and celery until they begin to brown. Add the zucchini and sauté lightly.

Add the raisins, capers, pine nuts, and black olives, stirring to combine. Add the crushed tomatoes and the fried eggplant.

Season the mixture with salt and pepper and cook over low heat, stirring occasionally, for 3 minutes.

Add the vinegar and sugar and, lastly, the pistachios and the basil; stir to combine.

To serve, spread the caponata on bruschetta or a sandwich, or offer as a side dish with fish or poultry.

Difficulty

FRIED MOZZARELLA CAPRESE
CAPRESE FRITTA

Preparation time: 25 minutes + 5 minutes cooking time

4 Servings

8 oz. (250 g) **fresh mozzarella cheese**
12 oz. (350 g) **tomatoes (about
  2 large)**
8 **medium fresh basil leaves**
1/3 cup plus 1 tbsp. (50 g) **all-purpose
  flour**
3 **large eggs, lightly beaten**
2 cups (275 g) **plain breadcrumbs**
Olive oil for frying
Salt to taste

Method

Slice the mozzarella and tomatoes to about 1/4 inch (1/2 cm) thick.

Using 2 slices each of tomato and cheese for each stack, alternate the tomato and cheese, inserting a basil leaf between layers. Wrap each stack in paper towels to absorb the excess liquid from both the cheese and tomatoes.

Place the flour, the beaten eggs, and the breadcrumbs in separate bowls. Remove the paper towels from the tomato stacks and dredge each stack in flour, then dip them in the beaten egg, and coat with breadcrumbs. Once more, dip the stack in the egg and coat in breadcrumbs, shaking off any excess.

Heat 1/2 inch of oil in a large skillet until shimmering. Using a slotted spoon, carefully transfer the stacks to the hot oil and fry for 30 seconds. Turn to fry on the other side for 30 seconds more.

Remove the stacks with the slotted spoon and transfer them to paper towels to absorb excess oil. Sprinkle with salt and serve.

Difficulty

PECORINO AND VEGETABLE STACKS

INSALATA PANE CARASAU

Preparation time: 30 minutes

4 Servings

6 slices carasau bread or other thin,
   crispy flatbread

5 oz. (150 g) cherry tomatoes, thinly
   sliced

5 oz. (150 g) shallots, thinly sliced

5 oz. (150 g) radishes, thinly sliced
   (about 1 1/4 cups)

5 oz. (150 g) cucumbers (about
   1/2 medium), peeled and thinly sliced

Salt and freshly ground black pepper
   to taste

3 oz. (90 g) Pecorino cheese, shaved thin

Extra-virgin olive oil

Chopped fresh chives for garnish

Method

Soak the flatbread in a bowl of water just until it begins to soften. Cut it into sixteen 2- to 3-inch (5-7 cm) rounds.

Place each of the vegetables in separate bowls, season to taste with salt and pepper, and drizzle with olive oil.

For each of the 4 stacks, you will use a quarter of the vegetables and 4 flatbread rounds.

Place 1 flatbread round in the center of each serving plate. Arrange one-quarter of the tomato slices on top of each flatbread so that they overlap slightly. Top each with another flatbread round and arrange the radish slices on top in the same manner. Top this with another flatbread round and a layer of the cucumber slices and the shallots, followed by a fourth flatbread round.

Scatter the shaved Pecorino on top and around the stacks. Drizzle with olive oil and sprinkle with chives.

Difficulty

GOAT CHEESE TARTELETTES

TORTA SALATA POMODORO E CAPRINO

Preparation time: 20 minutes + 30 minutes cooking time

4 Servings

7 oz. (200 g) **frozen puff pastry (about 1 sheet), thawed**

7 oz. (200 g) **tomatoes (about 2 medium), thinly sliced**

2 oz. (60 g) **soft goat cheese, thinly sliced**

1 tsp. **cornstarch**

2/3 cup (150 ml) **lukewarm milk**

1 **large egg**

2 1/2 tbsp. (15 g) **Parmigiano Reggiano cheese, grated**

Salt and freshly ground black pepper to taste

1 **bunch fresh chives, chopped**

Method

Heat the oven to 350°F (175°C).

On a clean work surface, roll out the puff pastry to about 1/8 inch (3 mm) thick. Line a 9-inch square baking pan with the pastry or cut into four 6-inch rounds to fit into four 6-inch ramekins.

Arrange the sliced tomatoes and goat cheese on the surface of the puff pastry.

In a medium bowl, dissolve the cornstarch into 1/3 cup of the milk. Whisk the egg, the remaining 1/3 cup milk, the Parmigiano, salt, pepper, and chives into the cornstarch mixture.

Pour the mixture over the tomatoes and cheese in the baking pan, or divide evenly among the ramekins.

Bake for about 25 minutes, or until the cheese is lightly browned. Serve warm.

Difficulty

CHICKPEA FLATBREAD

FARINATA

Preparation time: 10 minutes + 2 to 12 hours resting time + 20 minutes cooking time

4 Servings

3 1/2 cups (400 g) **chickpea flour**
4 cups (950 ml) **water**
Salt and freshly ground black pepper
1/2 cup (118 ml) **extra-virgin olive oil**

Method

In a large bowl, whisk together the chickpea flour and water. Season with 1/5 oz. (4 g) salt and allow to rest at room temperature for at least 2 hours or up to 12 hours.

Skim off any froth that has formed on the surface of the batter, then stir the flour mixture.

Heat the oven to 425°F (220°C). Prepare a large rimmed baking sheet by drizzling the olive oil to coat the bottom.

Pour the batter through a fine-mesh sieve onto the pan, making a layer about 1/4 inch deep.

Stir the batter with a wooden spoon to absorb the oil. Sprinkle generously with pepper.

Bake for about 20 minutes, or until golden-brown. Serve warm.

Difficulty

32

PARMIGIANO REGGIANO PINWHEELS

GIRANDOLE AL PARMIGIANO REGGIANO

Preparation time: 1 hour + 1 hour and 30 minutes rising time + 20 minutes cooking time

8 Servings

FOR THE DOUGH

4 cups (500 g) **Italian type "00" or all-purpose flour**
3/4 oz. (20 g) **sugar**
1 **large egg**
3/4 oz. (20 g) **active dry yeast, dissolved in 1 cup (250 ml) warm water (105°F / 40°C)**
1 oz. (25 g) **unsalted butter, softened, plus more for greasing pan**
Salt

FOR THE FILLING

1 **large egg, beaten**
1/2 cup (55 g) **Parmigiano Reggiano cheese, grated**

Method

On a clean surface, mound the flour, then form a well in the center. Add the sugar and egg to the well. Stirring, drizzle in the water in which the yeast has been dissolved. Add the butter and 1/5 oz. (4 g) salt, then knead the dough until it is smooth and elastic.

Place the dough in a large bowl. Cover the bowl with plastic wrap and allow the dough to rest at warm room temperature for about 30 minutes, until is has doubled in bulk.

Roll out the dough on a lightly floured surface to a rectangle about 1/8 inch (3 mm) thick. Lightly brush with the beaten egg, then sprinkle with the cheese. Starting at one long side, roll up the dough jelly-roll style. Cut the log crosswise into 3/4-inch (2 cm) pieces (refrigerate the remaining beaten egg).

Arrange the pieces cut side up on a greased baking sheet at least 1 inch (3 cm) apart and let rise at warm room temperature until doubled in volume, about 1 hour.

Heat the oven to 400°F (204°C). Brush the pinwheels with the remaining beaten egg and bake until lightly golden, about 20 minutes.

Difficulty

SUN-DRIED TOMATO AND CAPER TWISTS

NASTRINE CON POMODORI SECCHI E CAPPERI

Preparation time: 1 hour + 1 hour and 30 minutes rising time + 20 minutes cooking time

4 Servings

FOR THE DOUGH

4 cups (500 g) **Italian type 00 or all-purpose flour**

1 **large egg**

1 tbsp. plus 2 tsp. (20 g) **sugar**

1 tbsp. (8.5 g) **active dry yeast dissolved in 1 cup (250 ml) warm water (105°F / 40°C)**

2 tbsp. (25 g) **unsalted butter, softened**

2 tsp. (12 g) **salt**

FOR THE FILLING

2 oz. (60 g) **sun-dried tomatoes, chopped**

5 1/2 oz. (150 g) **capers, rinsed and desalted**

Dried oregano to taste

1 **large egg, beaten**

Method

On a clean surface, mound the flour, then form a well in the center. Add the egg and sugar to the well. Stirring, drizzle in the water in which the yeast has been dissolved. Add the butter and the salt, then knead the dough until it is smooth and elastic.

Place the dough in a large bowl. Cover the bowl with plastic wrap and allow the dough to rest at warm room temperature for about 30 minutes, until it has doubled in bulk.

Meanwhile, in a bowl, mix together the sun-dried tomatoes and capers. Add oregano to taste; set aside.

Roll out the dough on a lightly floured surface to a rectangle about 1/8 inch (3 mm) thick. Lightly brush with the beaten egg, then sprinkle with the sun-dried tomato mixture. Starting at one long side, fold the dough in half, then cut it into 1 1/2-inch (3 cm) wide strips. Wind the strips into twists and arrange them on a greased baking sheet at least 1 inch apart and let rise at warm room temperature until doubled in volume, about 1 hour.

Heat the oven to 400°F (204°C).

Brush the twists with the remaining beaten egg and bake until golden-brown, about 20 minutes.

Difficulty

PARMESAN SOUFFLÉS

SFORMATINI DI PARMIGIANO REGGIANO

Preparation time: 10 minutes + 30 minutes cooking time

4 Servings

1 cup (250 ml) **heavy cream**
1 1/4 tbsp. (10 g) **cornstarch**
1 tbsp. **lukewarm milk**
2 **large eggs, beaten**
3/4 cup (80 g) **grated Parmigiano
  Reggiano cheese**
**Salt and freshly ground black pepper
  to taste**
3/4 tbsp. (10 g) **unsalted butter**

Method

Heat the oven to 300°F (150°C). Heat the cream in a medium saucepan over low.

In a small bowl, dilute the cornstarch in the milk. Add it to the cream and stir to combine. Remove the pan from the heat and allow to cool for a few minutes.

Add the beaten eggs to the cream mixture, then add the grated cheese. Season with 1/5 oz. (4 g) salt and pepper.

Butter 4 small soufflé molds and divide the mixture evenly among them. Place the soufflé molds in a roasting pan filled with hot water that comes halfway up the side of the mold (or place in a bain-marie).

Bake until the soufflés are puffed and deeply browned, about 20 minutes. Don't open the oven door for at least the first 15 minutes.

Serve immediately; the soufflés will begin to collapse almost as soon as you take them out of the oven.

Difficulty

SQUASH-STUFFED MUSHROOMS

FUNGHI RIPIENI

Preparation time: 20 minutes + 20 minutes cooking time

4 Servings

10 1/2 oz. (300 g) **porcini mushrooms (ceps)**

2 tbsp. (25 ml) **extra-virgin olive oil**

10 1/2 oz. (300 g) **butternut or acorn squash, peeled, seeded, and cut into 1/8-inch (2 millimeter) cubes**

Salt and freshly ground black pepper to taste

2 oz. (50 g) **shallot, finely chopped**

1/2 **clove garlic, finely chopped**

1 **sprig fresh rosemary, leaves finely chopped**

1 **sprig fresh thyme, leaves finely chopped**

1 tbsp. **finely chopped fresh parsley**

1/2 cup (55 g) **grated Parmigiano Reggiano cheese**

Method

Heat the oven to 350°F (175°C).

Clean the mushrooms and pull the stems from the caps to make space for the stuffing. Cut the stems into cubes.

Heat 1 tablespoon of the oil in a large skillet over medium heat, then sauté the diced squash with salt and pepper.

Transfer the squash to a large plate. In the same skillet, heat the remaining 1 tablespoon oil over medium heat. Add the mushroom stems, shallot, garlic, rosemary, thyme, and half of the parsley. Cook for about 2 minutes, then return the squash to the pan. Stir to combine, then remove the pan from the heat and let the vegetables cool completely.

Add the remaining parsley and all but 1 tablespoon of cheese to the vegetables, then adjust the salt and pepper to taste.

On a baking sheet, turn the mushroom caps stem side up and mound the filling in the caps, then sprinkle with the reserved cheese. Bake until the mushrooms are hot throughout, about 10 minutes.

Difficulty

SOUPS

CHAPTER TWO

MINESTRONE
MINESTRONE

Preparation time: 20 minutes + overnight soaking + 1 hour cooking time

4 Servings

4 oz. (100 g) dried borlotti beans
  (cranberry beans) (1/2 cup)

4 oz. (100 g) dried cannellini beans
  (1/2 cup)

8 1/2 cups (2 l) water

1/3 cup (80 ml) extra-virgin olive oil

3 oz. (90 g) leeks (white and light
  green parts of 1 small leek), chopped

3 oz. (70 g) celery (about 3 stalks),
  thinly sliced

7 oz. (200 g) potatoes (about
  1 1/2 medium), diced

5 oz. (150 g) zucchini (about
  1/2 medium), diced

4 oz. (100 g) butternut or acorn
  squash, peeled and diced

4 oz. (100 g) savoy cabbage, coarsely
  chopped

4 oz. (100 g) green beans, cut into
  1-inch lengths (3 cm)

3 oz. (80 g) carrots (about 1 medium),
  peeled and diced

Salt to taste

1/2 bunch fresh parsley, some leaves
  left whole and some chopped

Parmigiano Reggiano cheese, shaved,
  for garnish

Method

Soak the borlotti and cannellini beans separately in cold water overnight; drain.

Combine the drained beans in a large saucepan. Add cold water to cover by 2 inches (5 cm). Bring to a boil, then reduce to a gentle simmer. Cook until the beans are almost tender, about 40 minutes; drain.

Meanwhile, bring the 8 1/2 cups of water to a boil in a saucepan.

In a large skillet, heat half of the oil over medium heat. Add the vegetables and cook, stirring occasionally, for 4 to 5 minutes.

Transfer the vegetables to the boiling water and bring back to a boil, then reduce to a simmer and cook for 50 minutes.

Add the cooked beans and simmer for 10 minutes more. Season with salt to taste and sprinkle with the parsley.

Drizzle each bowl of soup with the remaining oil, garnish with Parmigiano, and serve.

Difficulty

CREAMY BROCCOLI SOUP WITH TOASTED BREAD AND WALNUTS

CREMA DI BROCCOLI CON PANE CROCCANTE E NOCI

Preparation time: 20 minutes + 45 minutes cooking time

4 Servings

1 lb. (500 g) **broccoli, coarsely chopped**

1 1/3 lbs. (600 g) **potatoes (about 3 medium), thinly sliced**

3 1/2 oz. (100 g) **onion (about 1 small), thinly sliced**

6 1/3 cups (1.5 L) **water**

Salt and freshly ground black pepper to taste

2 tsp. (10 ml) **extra-virgin olive oil, plus more for drizzling**

2 oz. (60 g) **cubed day-old bread (about 1 3/4 cups small cubes)**

8 **walnut halves, coarsely chopped**

Method

Combine the vegetables in a large saucepan. Add the water and bring to a boil. Reduce to a simmer and cook until the vegetables are tender.

In a blender, purée the vegetables. Return the purée to the saucepan and thin with a bit of water, if necessary, then season with salt and pepper to taste.

In a nonstick pan, heat the olive oil over medium-high heat. Add the bread and cook, stirring occasionally, until toasted. Meanwhile, gently reheat the soup.

Serve the soup with the toasted bread and walnut pieces sprinkled on top and drizzled with oil.

Vegetable soups

In the past, food was often a sign of individual identity and social belonging, and in some ways it still is. During the Middle Ages, the ecclesiastical category clearly demonstrated a person's alterity in comparison to others (through clothing and lifestyle). A monk's choice to follow a spiritual path, mortifying his body and denying himself all sensual pleasures, was even manifested in food. So vegetable soups, which were often made with vegetables grown in the monastery gardens by the monks themselves, became a fundamental meal in the cloistral life.

While the powerful flaunted their social status through food (abundant, rare, and original), farmers and the general population were left to a poor and simple diet without any choice in the matter. And in the middle, as far away and different from one end as the other, were the men and women of the church who renounced food as a sign of devotion. In short, as food historian Massimo Montanari emphasized, "even hunger became a luxury item" in the Middle Ages.

Difficulty

ROMAN EGG DROP SOUP

STRACCIATELLE ALLA ROMANA

Preparation time: 10 minutes + 10 minutes cooking time

4 Servings

4 **large eggs**

1/2 cup (55 g) **grated Parmigiano Reggiano cheese, plus more for serving**

4 1/4 cups (1 l) **vegetable broth**

Salt to taste

Method

In a medium bowl, whisk together the eggs and cheese.

Bring the broth to a boil in a medium saucepan. Whisking constantly to shred the eggs as they cook, add one-third of the egg mixture. In 2 batches, add the remaining eggs, whisking frequently and returning the soup to a boil between additions.

Once all the eggs have been added, bring the soup to a final boil, whisking to break up any large clusters of eggs, then remove the pan from the heat. Season the soup with salt to taste. Serve with additional cheese.

Difficulty

PASTA AND BEANS
PASTA E FAGIOLI

Preparation time: 20 minutes + overnight soaking + 1 hour cooking time

8 to 10 Servings

7 oz. (200 g) **dried white beans (scant 1 cup)**

1 1/4 lbs. (200 g) **dried cannellini beans (scant 2 cups)**

7 oz. (200 g) **dried borlotti (cranberry) beans (scant 1 cup)**

7 oz. (200 g) **onion (about 1 medium)**

3 1/2 oz. (100 g) **carrots (about 2 small)**

3 1/2 oz. (100 g) **celery stalks (about 4 stalks)**

2 tbsp. (30 ml) **extra-virgin olive oil**

Leaves from 1 sprig fresh thyme

2 **bay leaves**

Salt and freshly ground black pepper to taste

5 oz. (150 g) **ditalini pasta**

Method

Soak the cannellini beans and borlotti beans in a large pot of cold water to cover by 2 inches overnight; drain.

Finely chop the onion, carrots, and celery.

Heat the oil in a large pot over medium heat, sauté the vegetables, then add the drained beans, thyme, and bay leaves. Add cold water to cover the beans by 2 inches. Bring to a boil, then reduce to a simmer and cook, adding more water if necessary to keep the beans covered until the beans are tender, anywhere from 45 to 90 minutes (depending on the freshness of the beans).

Ten minutes before the beans are cooked, season with salt and pepper, then stir in the ditalini and continue cooking until the pasta is al dente. Remove the bay leaves and serve.

Difficulty

EGGPLANT PURÉE WITH BARLEY AND ZUCCHINI

CREMA DI MELANZANE

Preparation time: 30 minutes + 50 minutes cooking time

4 Servings

1 **medium eggplant**
Salt and freshly ground black pepper
2 1/2 tbsp. (30 ml) **extra-virgin olive oil**
1 **small onion, finely chopped**
1 **clove garlic**
1 oz. (28 g) **finely chopped fresh sage, thyme, and rosemary**
1 **small potato, peeled and thinly sliced**
6 1/3 cups (1 1/2 l) **vegetable broth, heated to a boil**
1 cup (200 g) **pearl barley**
Vegetable oil for frying (optional)
1 **small zucchini, diced**

Method

Peel the eggplant (reserving the peel for garnish, if desired), then dice. Put the eggplant in a colander, salt it lightly, and allow it to drain for about 30 minutes.

Heat 2 tablespoons of the olive oil in a large wide saucepan and sauté the onion, garlic, and herbs. Add the eggplant and cook until lightly golden then add the potato.

Season with salt and pepper, then add 6 cups of the broth. Bring to a simmer and cook until the vegetables are tender.

In batches, purée the mixture in a blender. Return the purée to the pot, then stir in the barley. Bring the soup to a simmer and cook, adding more broth to thin the soup, if necessary, until the barley is tender, about 40 minutes.

Meanwhile, thinly slice the reserved eggplant peel lengthwise, if you want to fry it for garnish. In a large skillet, heat 1/2 inch of vegetable oil over high heat until shimmering. Fry the peel until golden. Using a slotted spoon, transfer the fried peel to paper towels to drain. Season with salt to taste.

In a small skillet, heat the remaining 1/2 tablespoon of olive oil over medium heat. Sauté the zucchini until tender and lightly golden, then remove the pan from the heat.

Stir the zucchini into the finished soup. Serve, garnished with the fried eggplant peel, if using.

Difficulty

BREAD AND TOMATO SOUP

PAPPA DI POMODORO

Preparation time: 10 minutes + 50 minutes cooking time

4 Servings

1 lb. (500 g) **tomatoes**
1/3 cup plus 1 1/2 tbsp. (100 ml) **extra-
  virgin olive oil**
1 **medium onion, thinly sliced**
3 **cloves garlic**
1/2 tsp. **chili powder**
1 cup (250 ml) **water**
**Salt and freshly ground black pepper
  to taste**
1-lb. (500 g) **loaf day-old rustic-style
  bread, diced**
20 **leaves fresh basil, torn**

Method

Bring a large pot of water to a boil. Make an X-shaped incision on the bottom of each tomato and blanch them in boiling water for 10 to 15 seconds. Immediately submerge them in ice water, then peel, core, and cut them into 4 sections.

Remove and discard the tomato seeds, then process the pulp in a blender. Set aside the resulting sauce.

Heat 1/3 cup of the olive oil in a large pot over medium heat. Sauté the onion, garlic, and chili powder until the vegetables are tender.

Add the tomato sauce and water and season with salt and pepper. Cover and cook the soup over low heat for 25 to 30 minutes.

Toast the bread in a large nonstick skillet over low heat. Remove the garlic from the soup, then stir in the toasted bread and the basil. Remove the soup from the heat. Cover the pot and let stand until the bread is softened, about 10 minutes.

Serve the soup warm, drizzled with the remaining oil.

Difficulty

CHICKPEA SOUP
MINESTRA DI CECI

Preparation time: 10 minutes + 12 hours soaking time + 1 hour 30 minutes cooking time

4 Servings

14 oz. (400 g) **dried chickpeas (about 2 cups)**
1 **medium onion, thinly sliced**
3 1/2 tbsp. (50 ml) **extra-virgin olive oil, plus more for drizzling**
1 **small bunch of sage, half left whole and half sliced**
8 1/2 cups (2 l) **vegetable broth**
Salt and freshly ground black pepper to taste
1/3 cup plus 1 tbsp. (40 g) **grated Parmigiano Reggiano cheese**

Method

Soak the chickpeas in cold water to cover by 2 inches for 12 hours. Drain, then put them in a pot with the onion, olive oil, and a few sage leaves. Stir to combine, then add the broth. Bring to a boil, then reduce to a very gentle simmer and cook for 1 1/2 hours.

Season the soup with salt to taste. If you prefer a creamier consistency, purée about a third of the chickpeas, then stir them back into the soup.

Serve with grated Parmigiano, freshly ground black pepper, and a drizzle of olive oil.

Chickpeas

Like all legumes of Eurasian origin, chickpeas have been eaten for tens of thousands of years. The classical period was their golden age. They were already highly appreciated by the Greeks, and the Romans also ate them in many different ways. The poet Horace confirms that his contemporaries were very fond of a sort of "chickpea cake" that was sold by street vendors, who did very good business. But the ancient Romans also ate these legumes boiled or roasted, the way we often eat peanuts.
But soup is definitely the dish that best represents chickpeas. Every region of Italy still has its own recipe for this substantial specialty (relatively simple, with one or more ingredients added), which has served as a daily meal for farmers over the last few centuries. Chickpea soup could probably be called the queen of traditional Italian popular dishes.

Difficulty

POTATO SOUP WITH SAFFRON
MINESTRA DI PATATE ALLO ZAFFERANO

Preparation time: 10 minutes + 40 minutes cooking time

6 Servings

1/4 cup plus 1 tsp. (70 ml) **extra-virgin olive oil**

1 **small onion, chopped**

1 **medium carrot, peeled and chopped**

1 **celery stalk, chopped**

3/4 tsp. **saffron threads**

1 1/3 lbs. (600 g) **small to medium potatoes**

8 1/2 cups (2 l) **water**

Salt

11 oz. (300 g) **cannarozzetti or flat wide pasta noodles, broken into small pieces**

Method

Heat the oil in a large saucepan over medium heat. Sauté the onion, carrot, and celery until tender. Stir in the saffron. Remove from the heat and set aside.

In a medium saucepan of boiling salted water, cook the potatoes until tender, about 15 minutes, then drain.

When the potatoes are cool enough to handle, peel and cut them into medium dice. Add them, along with the 8 1/2 cups (2 l) of water, to the vegetable mixture. Season with salt. Bring the mixture to a boil, add the pasta, and simmer until the pasta is al dente.

Remove the pot from the heat and let the soup stand for 5 to 10 minutes before serving.

Difficulty

POTATO AND CHESTNUT SOUP

ZUPPA DI PATATE E CASTAGNE

Preparation time: 20 minutes + overnight soaking +1 hour and 20 minutes cooking time

4 to 6 servings

7 oz. (200 g) **dried chestnuts**

2 1/2 tbsp. (35 g) **unsalted butter**

2 oz. (50 g) **leeks (whites only), finely chopped**

4 oz. (100 g) **onion (1 small), finely chopped**

1/2 lb. (250 g) **potatoes, peeled and diced**

4 1/4 cups (1 l) **vegetable broth**

2 cups (500 ml) **whole milk**

Salt and freshly ground black pepper to taste

1/2 **baguette**

Extra-virgin olive oil for drizzling

Method

Soak the dried chestnuts in cold water overnight; drain.

Melt the butter in a large saucepan over medium heat. Add the leeks and onion and sauté until lightly golden. Add the potatoes and chestnuts and sauté briefly, then add the broth and milk. Season with salt and pepper. Simmer very gently for 1 1/4 hours.

Meanwhile, cut the baguette into 1/2-inch slices (1 per serving), and lightly toast.

In batches, purée the pan contents in a blender until smooth, or, if you prefer a more rustic soup, leave it as is.

Serve topped with the toasts and a drizzle of olive oil.

Difficulty

PASTA & RICE

CHAPTER THREE

SPAGHETTI WITH CHEESE AND PEPPER

SPAGHETTI CACIO E PEPE

Preparation time: 10 minutes + 11 minutes cooking time

4 Servings

Salt and coarsely ground black pepper
12 oz. (350 g) **spaghetti**
2 1/4 cups (200 g) **grated Pecorino
   Romano**
1/2 cup (100 ml) **extra-virgin olive oil**

Method

Bring a large pot of salted water to a boil. Cook the spaghetti until it is al dente. Reserving 3 tablespoons of pasta cooking liquid, drain the pasta.

Mix the Pecorino with the olive oil and 2 to 3 tablespoons of the pasta cooking liquid in a large bowl. Toss the pasta with the Pecorino mixture. Season with salt and pepper to taste.

Difficulty

CAVATELLI WITH ARUGULA AND POTATOES

CAVATELLI, RUGHETTA, E PATATE

Preparation time: 20 minutes + 20 minutes cooking time

4 Servings

5 oz. (150 g) **arugula, plus more for garnish**

Salt and freshly ground black pepper to taste

5 oz. (150 g) **potatoes, peeled and cut into 1/2-inch dice**

14 oz. (350 g) **cavatelli**

2 tbsp. plus 1 tsp. (30 ml) **extra-virgin olive oil**

1 **clove garlic, thinly sliced**

5 1/2 oz. (150 g) **tomatoes (fresh or whole canned), chopped**

4 **leaves fresh basil, chopped**

Method

Rinse and dry the arugula.

Bring a large pot of salted water to a boil and cook the potatoes for 4 to 5 minutes.

Add the cavatelli to the pot and cook until it is al dente.

Meanwhile, heat 2 tablespoons of olive oil in a large pot over medium heat and sauté the garlic. Add a third of the arugula and sauté for 1 minute. Add the tomatoes, season with salt and pepper, and reduce the heat to low.

Drain the pasta and potatoes, then transfer to the pan with the sauce and stir well over low heat for a few minutes.

Add the remaining arugula and remaining 1 tablespoon of oil and toss. Sprinkle with the basil.

Difficulty

CASTELLANE WITH ARTICHOKES AND PECORINO

CASTELLANE CON CARCIOFI E PECORINO

Preparation time: 30 minutes + 25 minutes cooking time

4 Servings

4 medium artichokes
Juice of 1 lemon
3 tbsp. (40 ml) extra-virgin olive oil
2 oz. (60 g) shallots, thinly sliced
1 clove garlic, chopped
1 oz. (30 g) parsley, finely chopped
3 1/2 tbsp. (50 ml) dry white wine
Salt to taste
Crushed red pepper flakes
3 1/2 tbsp. (50 ml) vegetable broth
12 oz. (350 g) castellane (or penne rigate)
2 oz. (60 g) aged Pecorino cheese, shaved into thin slices

Method

Clean the artichokes by slicing at least 1/4 inch (1/2 cm) off the tops and bottoms and removing all the tough outer leaves.

Cut the artichokes in half lengthwise and remove the chokes. Cut into thin slices and soak in a bowl of water with the lemon juice to prevent the artichokes from discoloring.

In a large skillet, gently sauté the drained artichoke slices in the oil over low heat, with the shallots, garlic, parsley, and wine. Add the salt and crushed red pepper to taste. Cook until the wine evaporates, then add the broth and cook for about 10 minutes more.

Bring a large pot of salted water to a boil. Cook the pasta until it is al dente; drain, then toss with the sauce. Serve with the Pecorino on top.

Difficulty

FARFALLE WITH EGGPLANT SAUCE

FARFALLE ALLA CREMA DI MELANZANE

Preparation time: 5 minutes + 25 minutes cooking time

4 Servings

Salt and freshly ground black pepper
  to taste
1 1/2 lbs. (700 g) **eggplant**
1 **bunch fresh basil**
Vegetable oil for frying (optional)
12 oz. (300 g) **farfalle (bow tie pasta)
  or fusilli**
2 tbsp. (30 ml) **extra-virgin olive oil**

Method

Bring a large pot of salted water to a boil. Meanwhile, peel the eggplant (reserving some of the peel for a garnish, if desired) and cut it into a large dice.

Cook the eggplant in the boiling water for about 10 minutes, or until softened. Drain the eggplant.

Using a blender, purée the eggplant with the basil and a pinch of salt and pepper until a thick sauce forms.

Bring another large pot of salted water to a boil.

Meanwhile, thinly slice the reserved eggplant peel lenthwise, if you want to fry it for garnish. In a large skillet, heat 1/2 inch of vegetable oil over high heat until shimmering. Fry the peel until golden. Using a slotted spoon, transfer the fried peel to paper towels to drain. Season with salt to taste.

Cook the pasta until it is al dente. While cooking the pasta, warm the eggplant sauce over medium heat, adding salt and pepper to taste.

Drain the pasta and toss with the sauce and the olive oil. Serve, garnished with the fried eggplant peel.

Difficulty

FUSILLI WITH ARUGULA PESTO

FUSILLI CON PESTO DI RUCOLA

Preparation time: 15 minutes + 10 minutes cooking time

4 Servings

3 1/2 oz. (100 g) **arugula**

3/4 cup plus 1 1/2 tbsp. (200 ml)
  **extra-virgin olive oil (preferably
  Ligurian), plus more for drizzling**

1 1/2 tbsp. (10 g) **pine nuts**

1/4 **garlic clove**

Salt to taste

3 tbsp. (20 g) **grated Parmigiano
  Reggiano**

10 1/2 oz. (300 g) **fusilli bucati corti or
  fusilli**

Method

In a blender, combine the arugula, 2/3 cup (150ml) of the oil, the pine nuts, garlic, and a pinch of salt; purée until smooth. Transfer the pesto to a bowl; stir in the cheese, then cover with the remaining oil.

In a large pot of boiling salted water, cook the pasta until al dente. Reserving 1/3 cup of the pasta cooking liquid, drain the pasta, then transfer to a large serving bowl. Add the pesto and toss to combine, diluting the sauce with the reserved cooking liquid, little by little and as needed, and a drizzle of oil.

Difficulty

Chef's Tip

This recipe can also be made with farfalle (bowtie) pasta.

POTATO GNOCCHI WITH TOMATO AND BASIL

GNOCCHI DI PATATE AL POMODORO E BASILICO

Preparation time: 30 minutes + 1 hour and 15 minutes cooking time

4 Servings

FOR THE GNOCCHI

1 3/4 lbs. (800 g) **Russet potatoes**

1 1/2 cups (200 g) **Italian "00" flour or
all-purpose flour, sifted**

1 **large egg**

Salt to taste

FOR THE TOMATO SAUCE

2 1/2 lbs. (1.2 kg) **ripe tomatoes
(about 6 1/2 large)**

5 1/2 oz. (150 g) **onion (about
1 small), finely chopped**

3 1/2 tbsp. (50 ml) **extra-virgin olive oil**

1 **bunch fresh basil, leaves torn into
small pieces**

Salt

1 1/4 tsp. (5 g) **sugar (optional)**

1/3 cup plus 1 tbsp. (40 g) **grated
Parmigiano Reggiano cheese**

SPECIAL EQUIPMENT:

a potato ricer or food mill

Method

Cover the potatoes by 3 inches of cold water in a large saucepan. Bring to a boil; cook, uncovered, until the potatoes are tender, 25 to 30 minutes.

While they are hot, peel the potatoes using a paring knife; discard the skins. Cut the potatoes into quarters; in batches, pass them through a potato ricer or food mill onto a clean work surface. Combine the flour with the warm potato, adding the egg and a pinch of salt. Work into a dough with your hands, then knead once or twice just until smooth.

Dust a clean work surface and a baking sheet with flour. Cut the warm gnocchi dough into 6 pieces. Roll each piece between your hands and the work surface into a 1/2-inch-thick rope (1.25 cm). Cut the ropes crosswise into 3/4-inch (2 cm) pieces Roll each piece over the back of the tines of a fork or a gnocchi board to create the characteristic ridges, then place the gnocchi on the prepared baking sheet. Set aside.

Rinse the tomatoes and remove the stems. Blanch the tomatoes (see p. 54), then cut them into quarters. Remove and discard the seeds.

In a large skillet, sauté the onion with 2 1/2 tablespoons of the oil over medium heat. Soon after, add the tomatoes and half of the basil. Let the sauce cook for 15 to 20 minutes, then remove the basil and process in a blender. Stir in the remaining 1 tablespoon of olive oil, then season with salt to taste. If the sauce is too acidic, add a pinch of the sugar to taste.

Bring a large pot of salted water to a boil. Meanwhile, return the sauce to the skillet and very gently warm it over low heat.

In two batches, cook the gnocchi in the boiling water. As soon as they float to the surface, use a slotted spoon to transfer them to the skillet with the sauce; add the remaining basil and toss to coat. Serve sprinkled with the grated Parmigiano.

Gnocchi

Though gnocchi are not considered "real" pasta, they remain ever popular as a first course. In the Middle Ages, these tiny balls of dough were made from flour or breadcrumbs mixed with eggs and cheese, then boiled in water. When potatoes were introduced to Italian gastronomic culture in the modern era, the starchy tuber became the fundamental ingredient for gnocchi dough. Even the name has changed over time – they were actually called maccheroni at first (a term derived from the word macco, which in turn came from ammaccato, meaning "crushed") and were a particularly popular item on the tables of southern Italian farmers.

Difficulty

SPAGHETTI WITH MARINATED CHERRY TOMATOES AND FRESH RICOTTA

SPAGHETTI CON POMODORINI E RICOTTA

Preparation time: 15 minutes + 30 minutes marinating time + 12 minutes cooking time

4 Servings

2 tbsp. (5 g) **chopped fresh herbs such as mint, chives, thyme, and parsley**
1 **bunch fresh basil, chopped**
10 oz. (285 g) **cherry tomatoes, quartered**
1 **clove garlic, peeled and crushed**
3 tbsp. (45 ml) **extra-virgin olive oil**
   Salt and freshly ground black pepper
12 oz. (350 g) **spaghetti**
2/3 cup (150 g) **fresh ricotta cheese**
1/3 cup (40 g) **grated Pecorino cheese**

Method

Place the chopped herbs in a large bowl. Add the tomatoes and garlic, then add the olive oil. Season with salt and pepper and toss to combine. Let marinate at cool room temperature for 30 minutes.

Bring a large pot of salted water to a boil. Cook the spaghetti until it is al dente. Reserving 2 to 3 tablespoons of the cooking water, drain the spaghetti.

Sauté the pasta in a large skillet with the marinated cherry tomatoes, the ricotta, and the reserved pasta cooking liquid over medium heat for 1 to 2 minutes Sprinkle with the Pecorino.

Difficulty

Chef's Tip

Ripe cherry tomatoes give this dish lovely fresh flavor, and the sweetness of grape tomatoes is especially nice. Choose grape tomatoes, if they are available.

SQUASH RAVIOLI
CAPPELLACCI DI ZUCCA

Preparation time: 40 minutes + 1 1/2 hours resting time + 10 minutes cooking time

4 Servings

FOR THE PASTA

11 oz. (300 g) **all-purpose flour
(2 1/3 cups plus 1 Tbsp.)**
3 **large eggs**

FOR THE FILLING

2 1/4 lbs. (1 kg) **butternut squash,
peeled, seeded, and cut into 1/2-inch
dice**
Salt
7 oz. (200 g) **grated Parmigiano
Reggiano cheese**
1 **large egg**
Ground nutmeg

FOR SERVING

1 to 2 tbsp. **unsalted butter, melted**
Grated Parmigiano Reggiano cheese

Method

Make the pasta: Place the flour on a clean work surface and make a well in the center. Add the eggs to the well, and gradually mix with the flour, kneading until the dough is smooth. Let the dough rest for 20 minutes.

Make the filling: Put the squash, 2/3 cup water, and a scant 1/2 teaspoon salt in a large, deep sauté pan. Turn the heat to high until the water simmers; cover and steam the squash until it's just tender and the water has just evaporated, 5 to 6 minutes; check often. Drain.

Transfer the squash to large bowl. Add the Parmigiano and the egg. Mix until the ingredients are well combined. Season to taste with nutmeg and salt. Let the filling rest for 1 hour.

Using a rolling pin or pasta machine, roll the dough out into a thin sheet. Cut into 2-inch (6 cm) rounds or squares. Drop about 1 rounded teaspoon of the filling in the center of each square or round. Brush the edges of each with a little water. Top with a second pasta round, then push out any air bubbles and press the edges to seal completely.

Bring a large pot of salted water to a boil. Cook the ravioli until the pasta is cooked through and just tender, 3 to 4 minutes. With a large slotted spoon, transfer the ravioli to pasta plates.

Serve the ravioli drizzled with the melted butter and sprinkled with grated Parmigiano Reggiano. It is also delicious served with a bolognese sauce.

Difficulty

ORECCHIETTE PUGLIESE WITH BROCCOLI RAAB

ORECCHIETTE ALLE CIME DI RAPA

Preparation time: 5 minutes + 25 minutes cooking time

4 Servings

4 tbsp. (60 ml) **extra-virgin olive oil**
1 **clove garlic, sliced**
1 **red chile pepper**
**Salt and freshly ground black pepper
 to taste**
10 oz. (300 g) **orecchiette**
12 oz. (350 g) **broccoli raab, chopped**

Method

Heat 3 tablespoons of the olive oil in a large skillet and sauté the garlic and the whole chile over medium-low heat. Add 3 to 4 tablespoons of water. When the garlic is tender, remove the pan from the heat.

Bring a large pot of salted water to a boil. Cook the orecchiette for 7 to 8 minutes. Add the broccoli raab to the pasta pot and cook together until the pasta is al dente.

Reheat the garlic sauce for 2 minutes before draining the pasta and greens through a fine-mesh strainer. Remove the whole chile. Seed and slice the chile for a garnish, if desired.

Add the pasta to the garlic sauce and toss to combine, adding slices of chile, if desired. Season with freshly ground black pepper.

Difficulty

TRENETTE WITH PESTO
TRENETTE AL PESTO

Preparation time: 20 minutes + 20 minutes cooking time

4 Servings

1 oz. (30 g) **fresh basil leaves (about 1 1/2 cups)**

1/2 oz. (15 g) **pine nuts (about 2 tbsp.) plus more for garnish**

1 **clove garlic**

3/4 cup plus 1 1/2 tbsp. (200 ml) **extra-virgin olive oil**

Salt to taste

2 oz. (60 g) **Parmigiano Reggiano cheese, grated**

1 1/2 oz. (40 g) **aged Pecorino cheese, grated (about 1/3 cup plus 1 tbsp.)**

7 oz. (200 g) **potatoes (about 1 large), cut into small dice**

3 1/2 oz. (100 g) **green beans, finely chopped**

12 oz. (350 g) **trenette pasta or linguine fini**

Method

Rinse and gently dry the basil. In a mortar, pound the basil, pine nuts, garlic, 3/4 cup of the olive oil, a pinch of salt, and the grated cheeses (or blend the ingredients in a blender, using the pulse function to avoid overheating the pesto).

Transfer the pesto to a bowl and drizzle with the remaining 1 1/2 tablespoons of olive oil.

Bring a medium pot of salted water to a boil. Cook the potatoes and the green beans for 5 minutes. Add the trenette to the pot and cook until it is al dente. Reserving 1/4 cup of the cooking water, drain the pasta.

Transfer the trenette, potatoes, and beans to a large bowl. Toss with the pesto, diluting the mixture with a bit of cooking water and a drizzle of olive oil, if desired.

Garnish with pine nuts.

Difficulty

GNOCCHI FROM THE VALLE D'AOSTA
GNOCCHI DI PATATE ALLA BAVA

Preparation time: 5 minutes + 50 minutes cooking time

4 Servings

FOR THE GNOCCHI
1 lb. (500 g) **Russet potatoes**
Salt to taste
1 cup (125 g) **all-purpose flour**
1 **large egg**

FOR THE SAUCE
2 tbsp. (30 g) **unsalted butter**
5 oz. (150 g) **Fontina cheese, rind moved and cheese thinly sliced**
1/4 cup plus 3 tbsp. (100 ml) **whole milk**

SPECIAL EQUIPMENT:
a potato ricer or food mill

Method

Make the gnocchi: Cover the potatoes by 3 inches of cold water in a large saucepan. Bring to a boil; cook, uncovered, until tender, 25 to 30 minutes.

While they are hot, peel the potatoes using a paring knife or by rubbing the skin with your fingers; discard the skins. Cut the potatoes into quarters; in batches, pass them through a potato ricer or food mill onto a clean work surface. Combine the flour with the warm potato, adding the egg and a pinch of salt. Work the mixture into a dough with your hands, then knead once or twice just until smooth.

Dust a clean work surface and a baking sheet with flour. Cut the warm gnocchi dough into 6 pieces. Roll each piece between your hands and the work surface into a 1/2-inch-thick rope (1.25 cm). Cut the ropes crosswise into 3/4-inch (2 cm) pieces. Roll each piece over the back of the tines of a fork or a gnocchi board to create the characteristic ridges, then place the gnocchi on the prepared baking sheet. Set aside.

Cook the gnocchi and make the sauce: Bring a large pot of salted water to a boil. In two batches, cook the gnocchi in the boiling water.

While the gnocchi are cooking, make the sauce. Melt the butter in a skillet over low heat. Add the Fontina and the milk, and cook over low, stirring frequently to create a creamy sauce. As soon as the gnocchi float to the surface, use a slotted spoon to transfer them to the sauce. Toss to combine.

Difficulty

ORECCHIETTE WITH BROCCOLI, TOMATOES, AND ALMONDS

ORECCHIETTE CON BROCCOLI, POMODORINI, E MANDORLE

Preparation time: 10 minutes + 25 minutes cooking time

4 Servings

Salt and freshly ground black pepper to taste

12 oz. (350 g) broccoli, cut into small florets

2 tbsp. plus 1 tsp. (30 g) extra-virgin olive oil, plus more for drizzling

1 clove garlic, gently smashed and peeled

7 oz. (200 g) cherry tomatoes, cut in half

14 oz. (400 g) orecchiette

3 oz. (80 g) Pecorino cheese, shaved into small pieces

1 oz. (30 g) sliced almonds (about 1/4 cup)

Method

Bring a large pot of salted water to a boil. Add the broccoli and cook until crisp-tender, 3 to 5 minutes. Using a slotted spoon, tranfer the florets to a colander to drain. Reserve the boiling water.

Heat the oil in a large skillet over medium heat and sauté the garlic. Add the broccoli, then the tomatoes; reduce the heat to low and cook for 5 minutes. Remove the pan from the heat. Remove the garlic and discard. Season the vegetables with salt and pepper to taste, then drizzle with oil.

Cook the orecchiette in the boiling water until it is al dente. Drain the pasta, then transfer to a large serving bowl. Add the sauce and toss to combine. Serve topped with the cheese and almonds.

Chef's Tip

Because of their shape, orecchiette tend to clump together during cooking. To avoid this, stir the pasta constantly during the first few minutes of cooking.

Difficulty

GOAT CHEESE AND HERB RAVIOLI ("PIM") WITH BASIL PESTO

RAVIOLI DEL PIM CON CAPRINO, ERBETTE, E PESTO LEGGERO

Preparation time: 40 minutes + 30 minutes resting time + 5 minutes cooking time

4 Servings

FOR THE FILLING

3 oz. (80 g) **fresh ricotta cheese**

5 oz. (150 g) **soft goat cheese**

**Leaves from 1 sprig fresh marjoram,
chopped**

**Leaves from 1 sprig fresh thyme,
chopped**

2 **fresh basil leaves**

1 **large egg**

3 oz. (80 g) **Parmigiano Reggiano
cheese**

**Salt and freshly ground black pepper
to taste**

FOR THE PASTA

11 oz. (300 g) **all-purpose flour
(2 1/3 cups plus 1 Tbsp.)**

3 **large eggs**

FOR THE PESTO

3 tbsp. (40 ml) **extra-virgin olive oil**

1 oz. (30 g) **fresh basil (about
1 1/2 cups)**

3/4 oz. (20 g) **pine nuts (about 3 tbsp.)**

1 1/2 oz. (40 g) **Parmigiano Reggiano
cheese, grated (about 1/3 cup plus
1 tbsp.)**

3/4 oz. (20 g) **Pecorino
cheese, grated (about
1/4 cup)**

Difficulty

Method

Make the filling: In a large bowl, blend together the ricotta and goat cheese with a fork. Stir in the herbs, egg, and Parmigiano; add salt and pepper to taste.

Make the pasta: Place the flour on a clean work surface and make a well in the center. Add the eggs to the well, and gradually mix with the flour, kneading until the dough is smooth. Wrap the dough in plastic wrap and refrigerate for 30 minutes.

Flatten the dough with your hand, and run it through the widest setting on your pasta machine twice. Decrease the setting by 1 notch, then pass the dough through twice. Repeat this process until you can just see the shape and shadow of your hand through the dough sheet.

Cut the sheet in half crosswise and trim the sides to make two neat rectangles, one slightly larger than the other. On the smaller sheet, spoon mounds of 1 teaspoon of the filling, leaving 1/2 to 3/4 inch between each mound. Lay the second sheet of dough on top, draping it gently over the mounds without stretching it. Starting at one edge, gently press around each mound of filling to push out any air pockets and seal the sheets. Cut the pasta in between the mounds to form individual squares or circles with a scalloped pastry wheel, a ravioli stamp, or a paring knife. Press on the mounds to slightly flatten them and on the edges to seal.

Make the pesto: Combine all of the ingredients in the jar of a blender; purée until smooth, then transfer to a large wide bowl.

Bring a pot of salted water to a boil. Slide the ravioli into the water and cook until they float and are tender, 3 to 5 minutes. Working quickly, add 2 or 3 tablespoonfuls of the pasta cooking liquid to the pesto and stir to combine. Using a slotted spoon, transfer the ravioli to the bowl with the sauce, then gently toss to coat.

PAPARDELLE WITH MUSHROOMS
PAPARDELLE AI FUNGHI

Preparation time: 20 minutes + 15 minutes cooking time

4 Servings

Salt and freshly ground black pepper
  to taste
1 clove garlic, finely chopped
3/4 oz. (20 g) fresh parsley, finely
  chopped (about 1/3 cup)
2 tbsp. (30 ml) extra-virgin olive oil
14 oz. (400 g) mixed mushrooms, such
  as chanterelle, cremini, and oyster,
  trimmed and sliced 1/4 inch thick
10 1/2 oz. (300 g) papardelle or
  tagliatelle

Method

Bring a large pot of salted water to a boil.

Meanwhile, in a large skillet, sauté the garlic and parsley in the oil over medium heat. Add the mushrooms, increase the heat to medium high, and cook the until the mushrooms until they are tender but still slightly firm, about 5 minutes. Season to taste with salt and pepper, then remove the pan from the heat.

Cook the pasta in the boiling water until al dente; drain.

Return the pasta to the pot, then add the mushroom mixture. Toss to combine, cooking over low heat for 1 to 2 minutes.

Difficulty

CELLENTANI WITH TOMATO PESTO

CELLENTANI CON PESTO DI POMODORO

Preparation time: 10 minutes + 15 minutes cooking time

4 Servings

1 3/4 lbs. (800 g) **tomatoes**

2 oz. (60 g) **grated Parmigiano Reggiano cheese**

1 oz. (30 g) **pine nuts**

1 oz. (30 g) **blanched almonds**

1 oz. (30 g) **walnut pieces**

1 **clove garlic, minced**

5 **fresh mint leaves**

3 tbsp. (45 ml) **extra-virgin olive oil, plus more for drizzling**

Salt and freshly ground black pepper to taste

10 oz. (300 g) **cellentani pasta**

Method

Bring a large pot of water to a boil.

Make an X incision on the bottom of the tomatoes and immerse them in boiling water for 30 to 40 seconds, then remove them with a slotted spoon. Reserve the water for cooking the pasta. Allow the tomatoes to cool in cold water for 1 to 2 minutes, then drain, peel, and quarter them. Remove and discard the seeds and then cut the tomatoes into cubes.

In the jar of a blender, combine the tomatoes, cheese, pine nuts, almonds, walnuts, garlic, mint, and 2 tablespoons of the oil. Purée until smooth, then season to taste with salt and pepper.

Return the pot of water to a boil. Stir in the salt, then add the pasta and cook until al dente. Meanwhile, transfer the pesto to a large serving bowl.

Drain the pasta, then add it to the bowl with the pesto. Add the remaining tablespoon oil and toss to combine. Serve with a drizzle of olive oil and, if desired, another sprinkling of pepper.

Difficulty

Chef's Tip

This recipe can also be used with bavette pasta.

CAVATELLI WITH FAVA BEAN PURÉE AND CRISPY BREADCRUMBS

CAVATELLI CON PURÈ DI FAVE E PANE CROCCANTE

Preparation time: 20 minutes + 40 minutes cooking time

4 Servings

1 lb. (500 g) **shelled fresh or thawed frozen fava beans**
Salt
1 **small onion, finely chopped**
3 1/2 tbsp. (50 ml) **extra-virgin olive oil**
6 1/3 cups (1.5 l) **vegetable broth, heated to a simmer**
10 1/2 oz. (300 g) **cavatelli pasta**
3 1/2 oz. (100 g) **day-old bread, torn into coarse crumbs**

Method

If using fresh fava beans, cook in a large pot of boiling salted water until just tender, about 2 minutes (do not cook frozen beans). Using a slotted spoon, transfer to a colander set into a bowl of ice water (reserve the boiling water for cooking the pasta). Drain, then peel the beans (frozen beans will come pre-peeled).

In a large saucepan, sauté the onion with 1 1/2 tablespoons of the oil. Add the fava beans and gently sauté for a few minutes. Cover with the hot broth. Add a pinch of salt. Simmer for 30 minutes.

Transfer the beans with their broth to the jar of a blender and purée until smooth. Transfer the purée to a large wide serving bowl.

Return the water to a boil, add the pasta, and cook until al dente.

Meanwhile, in a large skillet, heat the remaining 2 tablespoons oil over medium-high heat. Add the bread and cook, stirring occasionally, until golden and crisp. Remove from the heat.

Drain the pasta, then add to the bowl with the cream. Toss to combine. Serve sprinkled with the breadcrumbs.

Difficulty

Chef's Tip

Orecchiette pasta can also be used in this recipe.

FETTUCCINE IN VEGETABLE RAGÙ
FETTUCCINE AL RAGÙ DI VERDURE

Preparation time: 1 hour + 20 minutes cooking time

4 Servings

FOR THE PASTA (SEE NOTE)

2 cups plus 3 tbsp. (300 g) **Italian "00" flour or all-purpose flour**

3 **large eggs**

FOR THE SAUCE

2/3 cup (50 g) **diced eggplant**

Salt and freshly ground black pepper to taste

1 **medium tomato**

1/4 cup (25 g) **shelled peas**

1 **small leek, white and light green parts only, thinly sliced**

3 tbsp. plus 2 tsp. (50 ml) **extra-virgin olive oil**

1 3/4 oz. (50 g) **red bell pepper, diced (about 1/2 small)**

1 3/4 oz. (50 g) **yellow bell pepper, diced (about 1/2 small)**

1 3/4 oz. (50 g) **zucchini, diced (about 1/2 small)**

1 3/4 oz. (50 g) **carrots, diced (about 1 small)**

1 3/4 oz. (50 g) **celery, diced (about 3 small stalks)**

6 **fresh basil leaves, roughly chopped**

NOTE:

1 lb. (450 g) of store-bought fettucine can be substituted for the fresh pasta in this dish, if desired.

Difficulty

Method

Make the pasta: Place the flour on a clean work surface and make a well in the center. Add the eggs to the well and gradually mix with the flour, kneading until the dough is smooth. Wrap the dough in plastic wrap and refrigerate for 30 minutes.

Flatten the dough with your hand, and run it through the widest setting on your pasta machine twice. Decrease the setting by 1 notch, then pass the dough through twice. Repeat this process until the pasta sheet is just under 1/16 inch (1 1/2 mm) thick. Cut the sheet into 1/4-inch (1/2 cm) wide strips.

Make the sauce: Put the diced eggplant in a colander, salt it lightly, and allow it to drain for about 30 minutes.

Meanwhile, bring a medium saucepan of salted water to a boil. Cut an X on the bottom of the tomato, then drop it in the boiling water for about 10 seconds. Using a slotted spoon, transfer the tomato immediately to cold water (reserve the water for the peas). Let stand for 1 to 2 minutes, then peel and cut into quarters. Remove and discard the seeds. Dice the tomato.

Boil the peas in the pot of salted water until tender. Drain, then rinse under cold running water and drain again.

Bring a large pot of salted water to a boil.

Meanwhile, in a large saucepan, sauté the leek in the oil until tender. Add the bell peppers and cook until tender. Add the eggplant, peas, zucchini, carrots, and celery; cook until tender. Season with salt to taste. Add the tomato and cook for a few more minutes until the flavors have blended, then stir in the basil. Remove from the heat.

Cook the pasta in the boiling water until al dente, then drain and transfer to a large wide serving bowl. Add the vegetable ragù and toss to combine. Serve with pepper sprinkled on top.

RISOTTO WITH ASPARAGUS
RISOTTO AGLI ASPARAGI

Preparation time: 15 minutes + 25 minutes cooking time

4 Servings

2 1/4 lbs. (1 kg) **asparagus**

Salt and freshly ground black pepper to taste

2 tbsp. plus 2 tsp. (30 g) **unsalted butter**

1 **small onion, finely chopped**

2 1/2 cups (500 g) **Arborio rice**

5 oz. (150 g) **Taleggio or similar cheese, crumbled**

Method

Fill a large saucepan with 7 cups water and bring to a boil.

Meanwhile, trim the asparagus, then remove and reserve the tips. Cut the stalks crosswise into 1/4-inch (1/2 cm) pieces.

Cook the asparagus (stalks and tips) in the boiling water with 2 teaspoons salt until crisp-tender, about 5 minutes. Using a slotted spoon or seive, transfer to a colander to drain. Reserve the asparagus water for cooking the rice.

In a heavy wide pot, heat 2 teaspoons (9 1/2 g) of butter over medium-low heat. Sauté the onion until translucent, 5 to 8 minutes. Add the rice, stirring to coat with butter, and cook until the rice is toasted. Increase the heat to medium and, in 1/2 cupfuls, add the hot water from the asparagus, stirring frequently and allowing the rice to absorb each addition of water before adding more. Do this until the rice is tender (you may have water leftover).

Add the asparagus, the remaining butter, and the cheese to the risotto. Stir together to combine, then season with salt and pepper to taste.

Difficulty

RISOTTO WITH CASTELMAGNO CHEESE

RISOTTO AL CASTELMAGNO

Preparation time: 5 minutes + 25 minutes cooking time

4 Servings

4 tbsp. (60 g) **unsalted butter**
1 **small onion, finely chopped**
1 1/2 cups (300 g) **Carnaroli rice or
   Arborio rice**
1/2 cup (100 ml) **dry white wine**
6 1/3 cups (1 1/2 l) **vegetable broth,
   heated to a simmer**
2 3/4 oz. (80 g) **Castelmagno or
   Gorgonzola cheese, coarsely grated**
Salt to taste

Method

Melt 1 1/2 tablespoons (20 g) of the butter in a wide heavy-duty 5- to 6-quart pot over medium-low heat. Sauté the onion until translucent, 5 to 8 minutes.

Add the rice and cook until toasted, stirring to coat the rice with the butter. Add the wine and cook over medium heat, stirring constantly, until the wine is absorbed.

In 1/2 cupfuls, add the hot broth, stirring frequently and allowing the rice to absorb each addition of broth before adding more. Do this until the rice is tender (you may have broth leftover).

Remove the pot from the heat, then stir in the remaining butter and the cheese, reserving a little bit of cheese for garnish. Season with salt to taste. Serve with the remaining cheese sprinkled on top.

Difficulty

RISOTTO WITH POTATOES AND LEEKS
RISO PATATE E PORRI

Preparation time: 10 minutes + 20 minutes cooking time

4 Servings

2 tbsp. (30 g) **unsalted butter**

1/4 lb. (120 g) **leeks, white and light green parts only, thinly sliced**

1 lb. (400 g) **medium potatoes, peeled and cut into 1/4-inch cubes**

1 1/2 cups (300 g) **Arborio rice**

1 1/2 quarts (1 1/2 l) **vegetable broth, heated to a simmer**

Salt and freshly ground black pepper to taste

Method

Melt the butter in a wide heavy-duty 5- to 6-quart pan and sauté the leeks over medium-low heat. Add the potatoes and rice and cook until the rice is toasted, stirring to coat with the butter.

In 1/2 cupfuls, add the hot broth, stirring frequently and allowing the rice to absorb each addition of broth before adding more. Do this until the rice and potatoes are tender (you may have broth leftover). Season with salt and pepper to taste.

Difficulty

BARLEY RISOTTO WITH GOAT CHEESE

ORZO CON LEGUMI ALL'OLIO D'OLIVA, FORMAGGIO DI CAPRA ED ERBE AROMATICHE

Preparation time: 30 minutes + overnight soaking time + 40 minutes cooking time

4 Servings

1 1/3 cups (250 g) **barley**

1/3 cup plus 1 1/2 tbsp. (100 ml) **extra-virgin olive oil**

10 **small spring onions or 1 small Spanish or yellow onion, diced**

2 **celery stalks, diced**

1 **small carrot, peeled and diced**

1/2 **small zucchini, diced**

10 **green beans, diced**

Salt and freshly ground black pepper to taste

5 cups (1 1/4 l) **vegetable broth, heated to a simmer**

8 oz. (240 g) **soft goat cheese**

1/4 cup plus 2 tbsp. (25 g) **minced fresh parsley**

1/4 cup plus 1 tbsp. (20 g) **minced fresh chervil**

3 tbsp. (15 g) **finely chopped fennel fronds**

6 to 7 **fresh chives, finely chopped**

2/3 cup (60 g) **grated Parmigiano Reggiano cheese**

Method

Soak the barley in a large pot of cold water overnight; drain.

Heat 2 tbsp. (30 ml) of olive oil in a large saucepan. Sauté the onion, celery, carrot, zucchini, and green beans. While the vegetables cook, add 2 to 3 tablespoons of the broth and season with salt.

Mix the goat cheese with 1 tablespoon (15ml) of the oil and a pinch of pepper; set aside.

Bring 4 cups (1 l) of unsalted water to a boil in a large pot. Add the barley and cook for 20 minutes, then drain and rinse under running water.

Heat 1 tablespoon (15ml) of oil in the pot, and return the barley to it. Continue cooking the barley, stirring until lightly toasted. As you would with risotto, gradually add the remaining broth, stirring frequently, until the barley is cooked and the broth is absorbed, about 10 minutes.

Stir in the vegetables, the remaining olive oil, the herbs, and the Parmigiano Reggiano, then season with salt to taste.

Divide between 4 shallow bowls. Top each serving with a dollop of goat cheese, a sprinkle of pepper, and a drizzle of olive oil.

Difficulty

MAIN COURSES

CHAPTER FOUR

TOMATOES STUFFED WITH RICE

POMODORI RIPIENI DI RISO

Preparation time: 5 minutes + 30 minutes cooking time

4 Servings

3 1/2 oz. (100 g) **Arborio rice (about 1/2 cup)**
Salt to taste
4 **medium tomatoes**
1/4 cup (60 ml) **extra-virgin olive oil**
3 1/2 tbsp. (20 g) **fresh oregano, finely chopped**
4 **fresh basil leaves, finely chopped**
1/2 **clove garlic, finely chopped**

Method

Heat the oven to 325°F (160°C).

Meanwhile, cook the rice in 1 cup of boiling salted water for 10 minutes. Drain, then spread on a large plate to cool.

Cut off and reserve about 1/8 inch from the the top of each tomato, then, using a small spoon, hollow out the bottoms. Finely chop the pulp. In a bowl, stir together the chopped pulp, oil, oregano, basil, garlic, and a pinch of salt. Stir in the cooled rice, then season the mixture with salt to taste.

Fill the tomatoes with the rice mixture, put the tops back on, and arrange them in a pan lined with aluminum foil. Bake for 15 to 20 minutes.

Remove the pan from the oven and let the tomatoes cool completely. Serve at room temperature or chilled.

Difficulty

ITALIAN WHITE BEANS WITH SAGE

FAGIOLI CON SALVIA

Preparation time: 10 minutes + 12 hours soaking time + 1 hour cooking time

4 Servings

14 oz. (400 g) **dried cannellini beans**

14 oz. (400 g) **tomatoes (about 4 medium)**

3 1/2 tbsp. (50 ml) **extra-virgin olive oil**

2 **cloves garlic**

Salt and freshly ground black pepper to taste

1 **sprig fresh sage**

Method

Place the beans in a pot of cold water to cover by 2 inches and soak overnight.

Bring the pot of beans and their liquid to a boil, then reduce to a gentle simmer. Cook for 30 minutes, or until the beans are tender yet still holding their shape, adding water if necessary to keep the beans covered by 1 inch.

Meanwhile, make an X incision on the bottom of each tomato. Blanch the tomatoes in boiling water for 10 to 15 seconds. Immediately submerge them in ice water, then peel, seed, and dice.

Drain the cooked beans. Heat the oil in a large skillet over medium heat, then add the garlic. Add the tomatoes and sauté for 10 minutes. Add the beans, season with salt and pepper, and cook for 10 minutes more. Remove the garlic, then garnish with the sage, whole or chopped.

Difficulty

BISMARK-STYLE ASPARAGUS

ASPARAGI ALLA BISMARK

Preparation time: 10 minutes + 20 minutes cooking time

4 Servings

1 3/4 lbs. (800 g) **large asparagus, trimmed**
Salt and freshly ground black pepper
1/4 cup (60 g) **unsalted butter**
4 **large eggs**
1/2 cup (50 g) **shaved Parmigiano Reggiano cheese**

Method

Cook the asparagus in a large pot of salted boiling water until crisp-tender, 7 to 10 minutes. Drain, then arrange on serving dishes.

Melt the butter in a large skillet. When it begins to foam, gently crack the eggs into the pan and gently cook them, being careful not to break the yolks.

Sprinkle Parmigiano shavings on the asparagus tips and arrange the eggs on top. Pour the hot butter over all. Season with salt and pepper to taste.

Freshly laid or mature?

Chicken eggs are used in cooking comprehensively all over the world. They are versatile, tasty, easy to digest, nutritious, and cheap. One of the ways to assess the quality of an egg is by its freshness; the fresher the better. A quick test to identify the age of an egg is to place it in a bowl of water. If the egg sinks then it's fresh, but if it floats then it's mature because the aging process causes the formation of air inside the egg. In China, however, mature eggs are a delicacy and even eaten when years old. Yes, years. The eggs are preserved for a few months in a mixture of wood ash, salt, lime, and clay. The result is an egg which lasts for ages!

Difficulty

EGGPLANT PARMIGIANA

MELANZANE ALLA PARMIGIANA

Preparation time: 30 minutes + 1 hour cooking time

4 Servings

1 1/4 lbs. (570 g) **medium eggplant, cut crosswise into 1/2-inch-thick rounds**

Salt to taste

2 3/4 oz. (80 g) **all-purpose flour (about 3/4 cup)**

2 **large eggs, beaten**

1 1/2 cups **vegetable oil, for frying**

11 oz. (300 g) **tomato sauce**

2 tbsp. (30 ml) **extra-virgin olive oil**

3 1/2 oz. (100 g) **fresh mozzarella cheese, crumbled**

3 1/2 oz. (100 g) **Parmigiano Reggiano cheese, grated**

Method

Put the eggplant in a colander, salt it lightly, and allow it to drain for about 30 minutes.

Heat the oven to 350°F (175°C).

Dredge the eggplant slices in the flour, then dip in the egg.

Heat the vegetable oil in a deep 12-inch skillet or wide heavy pot over medium-high heat until shimmering, then fry the eggplant 4 slices at a time, turning over once, until golden brown, 5 to 6 minutes per batch. Transfer with tongs to paper towels to drain. Season with salt.

Pour a thin layer of the tomato sauce over the bottom of a 9-inch (23 cm) square baking dish, then arrange a layer of the eggplant slices. Drizzle with a little bit of the olive oil. Cover with some of the mozzarella, then some more tomato sauce. Sprinkle with some of the Parmigiano Reggiano, then top with another layer of eggplant. Repeat the layering of ingredients, ending with a top layer of eggplant, covered with a little bit of sauce and cheese. Bake until bubbly and golden, about 25 minutes. Remove from the oven and let rest for 15 minutes before slicing.

King Parmigiano Reggiano

Of all the Italian cheeses, Parmigiano Reggiano is without a doubt the most well known throughout the world, fully deserving the title of "king" of cheese products. The different types of Parmesan are still made using a technique that was refined over centuries, which calls for a perfect balance between man, animal, and environment. Thanks to the monks who reclaimed the Po Valley and settled in the region, cattle breeding began on a large scale and allowed for large quantities of milk to be set aside for producing this aged, hard, "pasta cheese." It takes 158.5 gallons (600 l) of milk to make a single wheel.

Difficulty

ZUCCHINI WITH RICOTTA CHEESE

ZUCCHINE CON LA RICOTTA

Preparation time: 10 minutes + 30 minutes cooking time

4 Servings

Salt to taste
1 3/4 lbs. (800 g) **zucchini (about 4 medium)**
11 oz. (300 g) **fresh ricotta cheese**
1 **large egg**
1 **clove garlic, finely chopped**
1 tbsp. **finely chopped fresh parsley, plus more for garnish**
2 tbsp. (28 g) **unsalted butter, plus more for greasing**

Method

Heat the oven to 350°F (175°C). Bring a medium pot of salted water to a boil and cook the zucchinis (whole) until tender, about 3 to 5 minutes. Drain.

Trim the ends from each zucchini, then cut them in half lengthwise, and, using a small spoon, scoop out the pulp and discard it.

Using a rubber spatula, force the ricotta through a medium-mesh sieve into a medium bowl. Add the egg, garlic, and parsley; stir to combine.

Fill the zucchini halves with the mixture and arrange them in a buttered baking dish. Dot with the butter and bake for 15 to 20 minutes, until golden brown. Serve hot, sprinkled with parsley.

Difficulty

FRITTATA WITH POTATOES, ONIONS, AND ROSEMARY

FRITTATA CON PATATE, CIPOLLE E ROSMARINO

Preparation time: 10 minutes + 40 minutes cooking time

4 Servings

1 lb. (450 g) **potatoes**
1/2 lb. (225 g) **onions, thinly sliced**
3 tbsp. (40 ml) **extra-virgin olive oil**
Salt and freshly ground black pepper
8 **large eggs**
**Leaves from 2 small sprigs fresh
  rosemary**

Method

In a large pot of boiling water, cook the potatoes until tender when pierced with the tip of a paring knife. Drain and let cool, then peel and cut into small cubes.

In a large nonstick skillet, sauté the onion in half of the oil over medium-low heat until tender, about 10 minutes. Season with salt and pepper. Remove from the heat.

In a bowl, beat the eggs together with a pinch of salt and pepper and the rosemary. Stir in the potatoes and onions.

Return the skillet to medium heat. Add the remaining oil and heat until shimmering. Pour in the egg mixture, then reduce the heat to medium low. Cook the frittata until it begins to set, 5 to 8 minutes, then invert it onto plate. Slide it back into the skillet and continue cooking until the center is set, 5 to 8 minutes more.

Difficulty

ZUCCHINI PARMESAN
PARMIGIANA DI ZUCCHINE

Preparation time: 15 minutes + 1 hour cooking time

4 Servings

1 1/2 cups plus 1 1/2 tbsp. (20 ml)
extra-virgin olive oil

1 **clove garlic, peeled**

10 1/2 oz. (300 g) **crushed tomatoes**

**Salt and freshly ground black pepper
to taste**

1 1/3 lbs. (600 g) **zucchini (about 3
medium), cut crosswise into 1/8-inch
(3 mm) thick rounds**

1/3 cup plus 1 tbsp. (50 g) **all-purpose
flour**

2 **large eggs, beaten**

1/3 lb. (150 g) **fresh mozzarella, thinly
sliced**

1 cup (100 g) **grated Parmigiano
Reggiano cheese**

1 **small bunch fresh basil, leaves torn**

Method

In a medium saucepan, combine 1 1/2 tablespoons of the oil and the garlic. Heat over low heat for 3 to 4 minutes (do not brown the garlic). Add the crushed tomatoes and a generous pinch of salt and pepper. Gently simmer for 20 minutes.

Meanwhile, heat the oven to 350°F (175°C). Dredge the zucchini slices in the flour, then dip in the egg.

Heat the remaining 1 1/2 cups of olive oil in a deep 12-inch skillet or wide heavy pot over medium-high heat until shimmering. Fry the zucchini 8 to 10 slices at a time, turning over once, until golden brown, 1 to 2 minutes per batch. Transfer with tongs to paper towels to drain. Season with salt.

Remove the finished tomato sauce from the heat. Spread a thin layer of it in a baking dish. Cover with a layer of fried zucchini, then one of mozzarella. Follow that with another layer of tomato sauce. Sprinkle with some of the Parmigiano and some of the basil. Arrange another layer of zucchini. Repeat the layering of ingredients, ending with a top layer of zucchini, covered with a little bit of sauce and cheese.

Bake until bubbly and golden, about 25 minutes. Remove from the oven and let rest for 15 minutes before slicing.

Difficulty

CANNELLINI BEAN STEW

GUAZZETTO DI FAGIOLI CANNELLINI

Preparation time: 15 minutes + overnight soaking + 40 minutes cooking time

4 Servings

7 oz. (200 g) **dried cannellini beans**
2 tbsp. (30 ml) **extra-virgin olive oil**
1 tbsp. **finely chopped fresh parsley**
1 **clove garlic, finely chopped**
1 **sprig fresh thyme**
7 oz. (200 g) **tomatoes (about 2 medium), peeled, seeded, and cubed**
Salt and freshly ground black pepper to taste

Method

Place the cannellini beans in a pot of cold water to cover by 2 inches and soak overnight; drain.

Bring the pot of beans and their liquid to a boil, then reduce to a gentle simmer. Cook for 30 minutes or until the beans are tender yet still holding their shape, adding water if necessary to keep the beans covered by 1 inch. Drain the cooked beans.

Heat the olive oil in a medium pot over medium heat. Add the parsley, garlic, and whole sprig of thyme, then add the beans and the tomatoes. Season with a pinch of salt and pepper and cook for 5 minutes. Season with additional pepper to taste.

Beans in Italy

Before other species arrived from America, the only beans known in Europe were of the dolichos variety, called fagioli dall'occhio (eye beans) *in Italian for the small black spot where the seed is attached to the pod. The "poor man's meat," as legumes were once known, always played a fundamental role on the tables of the lower classes. In fact, it's worth noting that unlike other products from the Americas, beans spread quite rapidly throughout Europe. People were already used to eating them (mainly in soups, mixed with grains) and it wasn't difficult to integrate them into the existing gastronomic and agricultural systems.*

Difficulty

SPINACH AND SAGE GNUDI
GNUDI PROFUMATI AGLI ODORI DELL'ORTO

Preparation time: 30 minutes + 10 minutes cooking time

4 Servings

FOR THE GNUDI

Salt to taste
14 oz. (400 g) **fresh spinach**
7 oz. (400 g) **fresh ricotta cheese**
1 oz. (30 g) **Parmigiano Reggiano cheese, grated**
1 **large egg yolk**
1 cup (150 g) **all-purpose flour**
1/4 cup (40 g) **cornstarch**
Ground nutmeg to taste

FOR THE SAUCE

4 Tbsp. (60 g) **unsalted butter**
15 **fresh sage leaves**
Grated Parmigiano Reggiano cheese to taste
1/2 cup (100 ml) **tomato sauce**
4 **basil leaves for garnish**
Extra-virgin olive oil for drizzling

Method

Make the dumplings: Bring a pot of salted water to a boil. Cook the spinach until bright green, 3 to 5 minutes; drain and let cool completely. Squeeze well to extract excess water, then finely chop.

On a clean work surface, thoroughly combine the remainder of the ingredients with the spinach to create a soft, uniform dough. Let the dough rest for 15 minutes.

Using a pastry bag fitted with a 3/4-inch (2 cm) tip, form small logs of dough. Cut the logs into 1 1/4-inch (3 cm) dumplings.

Bring a large pot of salted water to a boil, and cook the dumplings until they rise to the surface. Using a slotted spoon, transfer the dumplings to plate. Drain off any excess liquid.

Make the sauce: In a large skillet, melt the butter with the sage leaves. Gently place the dumplings in the skillet, sprinkle with the Parmigiano, and gently toss to combine.

Heat the tomato sauce over medium, then divide among 4 shallow serving bowls. Arrange the dumplings on top and garnish with fresh basil leaves, if desired. Drizzle with oil.

Difficulty

SIDES & SALADS

CHAPTER FIVE

PANZANELLA

PANZANELLA

Preparation time: 15 minutes

4 to 6 Servings

2 1/4 lb. (1 kg) **rustic Tuscan bread, preferably day-old**
1 **clove garlic, minced**
1 tbsp. **capers, well rinsed and finely chopped**
1/2 tsp. (3 g) **salt**
Freshly ground black pepper to taste
1/4 cup plus 2 tbsp. (80 ml) **extra-virgin olive oil**
1 tbsp. (15 ml) **red-wine vinegar**
9 oz. (250 g) **bell peppers (about 2 medium), diced**
7 oz. (200 g) **tomatoes (about 2 medium), diced**
5 oz. (150 g) **red onions (about 2 small), thinly sliced**
4 oz. (120 g) **seedless cucumber (about 1 small), thinly sliced**
20 **fresh basil leaves**

Difficulty

Method

Cut the bread into 3/4-inch (2 cm) cubes, leaving the crust on.

In a large bowl, combine the garlic and capers. Add the salt and a pinch of black pepper, then the olive oil and vinegar. Mix together well, then add the bell peppers, tomatoes, cucumber, and onions. Mix again, making sure all of the ingredients are coated with the dressing.

Season the salad with salt and pepper to taste. Garnish with the basil.

Peppers

Peppers entered the Italian gastronomic system in the 16th century, along with other products from the Americas. The name of this vegetable probably refers to the distinctive spicy taste. Whether it was because of the particular flavor or the bright color, peppers were initially looked upon with mistrust, like many other plants that were unknown until that point. But contrary to many others, peppers were unexpectedly adopted by the masses (perhaps pushed by more urgent nutritional needs) before making their way to the tables of the aristocracy. The early tradition of pickling of peppers in vinegar (according to typical rural preservation methods) also points to the conclusion that the lower classes were the first to comprehend the taste and nutritional value of this succulent fruit of the earth.

BEET SALAD

INSALATA DI BARBABIETOLE

Preparation time: 10 minutes + 1 hour cooking time + 15 minutes marinating time

4 Servings

1 1/3 lbs. (600 g) **beets**
1/4 cup (60 ml) **extra-virgin olive oil**
1 tbsp. plus 1 tsp. (20 ml) **wine vinegar**
1 **clove garlic, peeled**
**Salt and freshly ground black pepper
  to taste**
7 oz. (200 g) **mixed salad greens**
1 cup (75 g) **slivered almonds**
1/2 cup (75 g) **chopped pistachios**

Method

Heat the oven to 400°F (205°C). Wrap the beets in aluminum foil and bake until they are easily pierced with a fork, about 1 hour. When the beets are cool enough to handle, peel and dice them into cubes.

In a large bowl, mix the beets with the olive oil, vinegar, whole peeled clove of garlic, and a pinch of salt and pepper. Allow to marinate for at least 15 minutes. Remove and discard the garlic.

Arrange the salad greens on serving plates and top with the beets. Garnish with almonds and pistachios and serve.

Difficulty

WARM GOAT CHEESE SALAD

INSALATA CON FORMAGGIO DI CAPRA TIEPIDO

Preparation time: 15 minutes + 6 to 8 minutes cooking time

4 Servings

8 (17- by 12-inch) **phyllo sheets, thawed if frozen**

1/3 cup plus 1 1/2 tbsp. (100 ml) **extra-virgin olive oil**

1 5-ounce (150 g) **log soft goat cheese, cut crosswise into 4 rounds**

8 oz. (225 g) **young salad greens**

1 tbsp. (15 ml) **balsamic vinegar**

Salt and freshly ground black pepper

Method

Trim the phyllo sheets into 8-inch (20 cm) squares. Lightly brush the tops with olive oil, then top with a second square and lightly brush with more oil. Repeat the process with the remaining squares.

Place a goat cheese round in the center of each phyllo stack, then fold and twist the phyllo around the filling to form bundles.

Heat the oven to 400°F (205°C) with the rack positioned in the middle. Bake the goat cheese bundles for about 8 minutes, until lightly golden. Alternatively, heat the 1/3 cup oil to 250°F (110°C) on an instant-read thermometer and fry the goat cheese bundles for 2 minutes.

Meanwhile, arrange the greens on serving plates. Drizzle with the remaining oil and the vinegar, and season with salt and pepper. Place a warm goat cheese bundle in the center of each salad and serve while the bundles are warm.

Difficulty

ASPARAGUS SALAD

INSALATA DI ASPARAGI

Preparation time: 25 minutes + 15 minutes cooking time

4 Servings

1 lb. (500 g) **asparagus**
**Salt and freshly ground black pepper
  to taste**
5 oz. (150 g) **radicchio, thinly sliced**
1/3 cup (80 ml) **extra-virgin olive oil**
1 oz. (30 g) **radishes (about 4), thinly
  sliced**

Method

Trim the asparagus. Thinly slice 2 of the spears and set aside for garnish.

Bring a large pot of salted water to a boil. Add the whole asparagus spears and cook until crisp-tender, about 10 minutes. Drain, cool, and halve the spears lengthwise.

Season the radicchio with salt and pepper, then drizzle with oil. Arrange the split asparagus and radicchio on serving plates, then garnish with the radishes and the reserved sliced asparagus.

Liquid gold

The olive tree (scientific name Olea europea*) is one of the most enduring images associated with the countries in the Mediterranean basin. The fruit from the tree is pressed to make olive oil. The most highly prized is known as extra-virgin olive oil which, according to the production regulations issued by the European Union in 2003, must comply with certain specific requisites such as using only oil obtained from the first press of the fruit and containing maximum acidity of 0.8%. Extra-virgin olive oil must also have specific sensory properties including a fruity aroma and a slightly bitter, spicy taste. Due to its nutritional content and taste, extra-virgin olive oil is undoubtedly the single best oil for use in cooking. It is delicious when used for dressings and excellent for frying as well as in the preservation of foods.*

Difficulty

MIXED SALAD WITH PINEAPPLE AND MELON

INSALATA MISTA CON ANANAS E MELONE

Preparation time: 30 minutes

4 Servings

1 ripe cantaloupe
1 ripe pineapple
Salt to taste
7 oz. (200 g) green beans
12 cherry tomatoes, stemmed and cut into quarters
1 green bell pepper, chopped
1/3 cup (80 ml) extra-virgin olive oil
Juice of 1 lemon
Tabasco sauce to taste
1 tbsp. (4 g) finely chopped fresh parsley, plus more for garnish

Method

Halve, peel, and seed the cantaloupe. Cube one half. Thinly slice the other half. Peel and core the pineapple and cut into 1-inch (3 cm) cubes.

Bring a medium saucepan of salted water to a boil and cook the green beans until crisp-tender. Drain well and then coarsely chop. Place in a large bowl. Add the cubed cantaloupe, pineapple, tomatoes, and bell pepper.

In a medium bowl, whisk together the olive oil, lemon juice, Tabasco sauce to taste, a pinch of salt, and the parsley.

Arrange the salad on serving plates and drizzle with the dressing. Garnish with the parsley and serve with the cantaloupe slices.

Difficulty

SPRING RICE SALAD

INSALATA DI RISO PRIMAVERA

Preparation time: 25 minutes +15 minutes cooking time

4 Servings

Salt to taste
1 scant cup (200 g) **Arborio rice**
5 oz. (150 g) **asparagus, trimmed and cut into 1-inch lengths**
4 oz. (120 g) **fresh shelled or frozen peas**
1 3/4 oz. (50 g) **squash blossoms, pistols removed, blossoms thinly sliced lengthwise**
1/3 cup plus 1 1/2 tbsp. (100 ml) **extra-virgin olive oil**

Method

Bring 2 medium saucepans of salted water to a boil.

Add the rice to 1 saucpean of boiling salted water and cook until tender, about 15 minutes, or for the time indicated on the package.

Meanwhile, cook the asparagus in the second saucpean of boiling salted water until tender, 7 to 8 minutes. During the final 2 minutes cooking time, add the peas. Drain the vegetables, then plunge into ice water to cool. Drain.

Drain the rice and rinse under cold running water, then place in a large bowl. Add the asparagus, peas, and squash blossoms. Season with a pinch of salt, then add the oil. Stir together well, then adjust the seasoning to taste.

Difficulty

FRESH VEGETABLE AND CORN SALAD

INSALATA DI MAIS

Preparation time: 10 minutes

4 Servings

1 16-oz. **can corn, rinsed and drained**

10 1/2 oz. (300 g) **bell pepper (about 2 medium), finely diced**

3 1/2 oz. (100 g) **cucumber (about 1 small), finely diced**

2 1/2 oz. (70 g) **celery (about 3 stalks), finely diced**

2 oz. (60 g) **scallions (about 4), white and light green parts only, thinly sliced**

1 3/4 oz. (50 g) **pitted olives, (about 12 large), chopped**

1/3 cup (10 g) **finely chopped fresh parsley**

1/3 cup plus 1 1/2 tbsp. (100 ml) **extra-virgin olive oil**

Salt and freshly ground black pepper to taste

Method

In a large bowl, mix together the corn, bell pepper, cucumber, celery, scallions, olives, and parsley. Drizzle with the olive oil. Season with salt and pepper to taste.

Tasty, nutritious, and healthy

Spring onions are the roots of onions which have not yet fully formed and are highly esteemed in cooking due to their versatility. They are excellent eaten raw, for example thinly sliced and added to a nice salad. They are also a tasty ingredient when used as the base for both simple and more complicated recipes. White spring onions have a strong flavor whereas the red variety is decidedly milder. Spring onions are packed full of nutrients including vitamins and mineral salts. They also aid digestion, act as a detoxification agent, and help to control blood glycemia, cholesterol, and triglyceride levels.

Difficulty

CAPRESE WITH SAUTÉED VEGETABLES

CAPRESE CON VERDURE SALTATE AL TIMO

Preparation time: 25 minutes + 15 minutes cooking time

4 Servings

3 oz. (80 g) **celery (about 3 stalks)**
3 oz. (80 g) **bell pepper (about
  1 small), seeded**
4 oz. (120 g) **zucchini (about 1 small)**
3 1/2 tbsp. **extra-virgin olive oil**
2 tbsp. (5 g) **fresh thyme leaves**
Salt and freshly ground black pepper
8 oz. (250 g) **ripe tomatoes**
12 oz. (320 g) **fresh mozzarella,
  preferably buffalo**
1/3 cup (10 g) **fresh basil leaves**
2 tbsp. (5 g) **fresh oregano leaves**

Method

Julienne the celery, bell pepper, and zucchini. Heat the olive oil in a large skillet over medium heat and lightly sauté the celery. Add the peppers and sauté for 2 minutes. Add the zucchini and the thyme and cook for 3 minutes more.

When the vegetables are cooked, season with salt and pepper. (Do not add salt and pepper before this point to prevent the vegetables from releasing moisture.)

Thinly slice the tomatoes and mozzarella. To serve, alternate slices of tomato and mozzarella on a plate. Place the sautéed vegetables and thyme in the center. Garnish with the basil and oregano.

Difficulty

GRAIN SALAD WITH VEGETABLES AND HERBS

INSALATA DI RISO, ORZO, E FARRO CON VERDURINE E ERBE AROMATICHE

Preparation time: 15 minutes + 45 minutes cooking time

4 Servings

Salt to taste
2 1/2 oz. (70 g) **rice (about 1/3 cup)**
2 1/2 oz. (70 g) **barley (about 1/3 cup)**
2 1/2 oz. (70 g) **spelt (about 1/2 cup)**
7 oz. (200 g) **eggplant (about
  1/2 medium)**
1 3/4 oz. (50 g) **celery (about 2 stalks),
  diced**
3 1/2 oz. (100 g) **leek (about 1 small),
  sliced (white part only)**
3 1/2 oz. (100 g) **zucchini (about
  1/2 medium), diced**
3 1/2 oz. (100 g) **red bell pepper (about
  1 small to medium), diced**
3 1/2 oz. (100 g) **yellow bell pepper
  (about 1 small to medium), diced**
5 oz. (150 g) **carrots (about 3 small),
  diced**
1/4 cup (60 ml) **extra-virgin olive oil**
2 **sprigs fresh thyme, leaves chopped,
  plus 4 springs thyme for garnish
  (optional)**
2 **sprigs fresh marjoram, leaves chopped**
2 **sprigs fresh sage, leaves chopped**
2 **sprigs fresh rosemary, leaves chopped**

Method

In separate pots of boiling salted water, cook the rice, barley, and spelt (per the package directions), each until al dente.

Drain well and spread the grains over a rimmed baking sheet to cool, stirring occasionally.

Meanwhile, dice the eggplant, lightly salt it, and allow it to drain in a colander for about 30 minutes.

In a large frying pan, sauté each of the vegetables separately with a little oil and the chopped herbs until crisp-tender. Season with salt, then add to a large bowl with the grains. Drizzle with the remaining oil, then season with salt to taste. Garnish with the thyme sprigs, if desired.

Difficulty

PINK GRAPEFRUIT, SPINACH, AND WALNUT SALAD

INSALATA DI POMPELMO ROSA, SPINACI NOVELLI, E NOCI

Preparation time: 20 minutes

4 Servings

2 pink grapefruit

2 oranges

2 lemons

1/3 cup plus 1 1/2 tbsp. (100 ml) **extra-virgin olive oil**

Salt and freshly ground black pepper to taste

7 oz. (200 g) **baby spinach, washed well and dried**

3 1/2 oz. (100 g) **coarsely chopped walnuts (1 cup)**

Method

Using a sharp paring knife, cut the peel and pith from the grapefruit, oranges, and lemons. Working over a bowl to catch the juices, slice between the sections and membranes of each fruit; remove the segments whole, reserving the fruit and juice.

To make the dressing, whisk the juices with the olive oil and a pinch of salt and pepper.

Arrange the spinach and the fruit segments on serving plates. Drizzle with the dressing and sprinkle with the walnuts.

Difficulty

Nutritious, but less than it seems

The best advertisement for spinach is undoubtedly Popeye, who has been using it since 1929 to acquire super strength. And it's true – this vegetable is nutritious and helps combat anemia. However scientific research has shown that even though spinach contains more iron than any other vegetable (2.9 ml per 3 1/2 oz. [100 g]), 95% of this mineral remains unused by the body due to the presence of oxalic acid, a substance which limits the bioavailability of minerals contained in green leaf vegetables.

VEGETARIAN COUSCOUS SALAD

INSALATA DI COUSCOUS VEGETARIANA

Preparation time: 15 minutes + 20 minutes cooking time

4 Servings

1 1/4 cups (300 ml) **vegetable broth or water**

1 cup (173 g) **dry couscous**

Salt to taste

2 oz. (60 g) **fresh shelled or frozen peas**

1 small (100 g) **red onion, finely chopped**

3 1/2 oz. (100 g) **zucchini (about 1/2 medium), cut into 1/8-inch (2 to 3 mm) dice**

2 oz. (100 g) **yellow bell pepper (about 1 small), cut into 1/8-inch (2 to 3 mm) dice**

3 1/2 oz. (100 g) **carrots (about 2 small), cut into 1/8-inch (2 to 3 mm) dice**

1/3 cup (80 ml) **extra-virgin olive oil**

2 tbsp. **finely chopped fresh parsley**

Method

In a small saucepan bring the broth (or water) to a boil. Stir in the couscous and let stand, covered and off the heat, for 5 minutes. Fluff the couscous with a fork and transfer to a bowl.

Bring a small saucepan of salted water to a boil. Add the peas and cook until just tender, then drain and rinse under cold running water. Set aside.

In a medium skillet, sauté each of the remaining vegetables separately in a little of the olive oil over medium heat until crisp-tender. Let the vegetables cool, then add them, with the peas, to the couscous. Drizzle with a little olive oil, then season with salt to taste. Stir in the parsley.

Difficulty

ZESTY CITRUS CHICKPEAS
INSALATA DI CECI

Preparation time: 20 minutes

4 Servings

1 lb. (500 g) **cooked chickpeas, rinsed and drained**
1/2 **yellow bell pepper, finely diced**
1/4 **red bell pepper, finely diced**
1/4 **red onion, finely diced**
1/4 **green apple, finely diced**
2 tsp. (10 g) **grated lemon zest**
2 tsp. (10 g) **grated orange zest**
2 tsp. (10 g) **grated lime zest**
1/3 cup (80 ml) **extra-virgin olive oil**
1 tbsp. (15 ml) **white-wine vinegar**
Salt and freshly ground black pepper to taste

Method

Mix together the chickpeas, bell peppers, red onion, apple, and zests in a medium bowl.

Drizzle with the olive oil and vinegar, then season with salt and pepper to taste. Toss to combine.

Chickpeas in the kitchen

After beans and soya beans, chickpeas (scientific name Cicer arietinum) are the world's most popular legume and have been eaten since ancient times. Chickpeas can be used in salads either on their own or with other vegetables. They must be soaked for 12-16 hours and then cooked in lightly salted boiling water flavored with bay leaf, rosemary, or sage. They can also be used for soups, pasta sauces, and as the main ingredient in classic Italian foods such as the "farinata" or "cecina" flatbreads originating in Liguria and Tuscany. Chickpeas are also the basic ingredient of hummus, the traditional Middle Eastern dip.

Difficulty

GRILLED POTATO STACKS

MILLEFOGLIE DI PATATE

Preparation time: 10 minutes + 20 minutes cooking time

4 to 6 Servings

1 1/3 lbs. (600 g) **potatoes (a mix of yellow, white, and purple potatoes)**
Salt and freshly ground black pepper to taste
3 1/2 tbsp. (50 ml) **extra-virgin olive oil**
Sprigs of fresh thyme
7 oz. (200 g) **tomatoes, diced**

Method

Boil the potatoes in a pot of salted water until tender but still firm, 12 to 15 minutes. Let them cool, then peel and cut them into 1/4-inch (1/2 cm) slices.

Transfer the potatoes to a very hot oiled grill or griddle, and cook the slices for about 4 minutes per side, until nicely browned grill marks appear. Season with salt, pepper, a drizzle of olive oil, and a few sprigs of thyme.

Assemble the stacks on a serving platter by layering the potato slices, alternating yellow, white, and purple potatoes. Garnish with the tomatoes and sprigs of thyme.

Difficulty

STUFFED ONIONS

CIPOLLE RIPIENE

Preparation time: 30 minutes + 40 minutes cooking time

4 Servings

3 1/3 lbs. (1.5 kg) **medium yellow onions, peeled**
1 **bunch fresh herbs (such as parsley, sage, rosemary, thyme, basil, and mint)**
7 tbsp. (100 g) **unsalted butter**
7 oz. (200 g) **fresh breadcrumbs (about 1 3/4 cups plus 1 tbsp.)**
1/2 cup (100 ml) **whole milk, plus more for egg mixture**
1 oz. (30 g) **raisins (2 rounded tablespoons)**
4 **large eggs**
7 oz. (200 g) **Parmigiano Reggiano cheese, grated (about 2 cups)**
Salt to taste

Method

Heat the oven to 350°F (175°C). Cook the onions in a pot of boiling water until tender, about 12 minutes. Remove them with a slotted spoon and allow to cool.

Cut a 1/2-inch-thick (1.25 cm) slice from the tops of the onions, discarding the tops, and trim just enough from the bottoms for the onions to stand upright. Scoop out all but the outer 2 or 3 layers from each using a small spoon (don't worry if you make a hole in the bottom), reserving the scooped out onion and onion shells separately.

Finely chop together the scooped out onion and the herbs. Melt 5 tablespoons of the butter in a medium saucepan and sauté the onion-herb mixture; season with salt.

Meanwhile, soak the breadcrumbs in the milk. Soak the raisins in warm water for about 10 minutes. Drain and squeeze out excess moisture from the breadcrumbs and raisins.

In a bowl, stir together the herb-onion mixture with the bread-crumbs, raisins, 2 eggs, and 1/2 cup Parmigiano. Stuff the boiled onions with the mixture. Arrange the onions in a lightly oiled baking dish.

Beat the remaining 2 eggs with the remaining 1 1/2 cups Parmigiano, adding 1 to 2 tablespoons of milk. Pour the egg mixture over the onions, then dot with the remaining 2 table-spoons butter.

Bake for about 20 minutes, or until the surface is golden-brown.

Difficulty

CAPONATA WITH FENNEL, OLIVES, AND RAISINS

CAPONATA CON FINOCCHIO, OLIVE E UVA PASSA

Preparation time: 30 minutes + 20 minutes cooking time

4 Servings

3 1/2 oz. (100 g) **raisins (about 2/3 cup packed)**

1 **small fennel bulb, thinly sliced (core removed)**

1/3 cup (80 ml) **extra-virgin olive oil**

1/2 lb. (225 g) **onions (about 2 medium), thinly sliced**

1 1/4 lbs. (565 g) **eggplant (about 1), cut into 1/2-inch (1 cm) cubes**

1 lb. (453 g) **red bell peppers (about 2 1/2 large), cut into 1/2-inch cubes (1 cm)**

2 **cloves garlic, sliced**

3 1/2 oz. (100 g) **oil-cured black olives, pitted (about 25)**

3/4 lb. (340 g) **tomatoes (about 1 1/2 large), seeded and cut into 1/2-inch cubes (1 cm)**

1/2 oz. (15 g) **basil (about 30 leaves)**

Salt and freshly ground black pepper to taste

1/3 cup (80 ml) **red-wine vinegar**

1/5 oz. (4 g) **sugar**

1 oz. (30 g) **pine nuts (about 3 1/2 tbsp.)**

Difficulty

Method

Soak the raisins in warm water for 15 minutes, then drain and squeeze out excess liquid.

Meanwhile, cut the fennel in half lengthwise; remove and discard the core. Thinly slice the fennel.

Heat the oil in a large skillet over medium heat and sauté the onion for 5 minutes. Add the fennel, eggplant, peppers, and garlic. Cook until the eggplant softens, about 10 minutes. Then add the raisins and olives, followed by the the tomatoes. Stir in two-thirds of the basil, 1/2 teaspoon salt, and a generous pinch of pepper. Cook, covered and stirring occasionally, for 5 minutes.

Add the vinegar and sugar to the vegetable mixture. Continue cooking, stirring occasionally, until the vegetables are tender.

Meanwhile, in a small skillet, heat the pine nuts over medium low, occasionally shaking the pan back and forth, until they're fragrant and lightly golden. Transfer to a plate to cool.

Stir the remaining basil into the finished dish, then sprinkle with the nuts.

Caponata

Like every classic recipe that's deeply rooted in the history of a region and its people, there are dozens of caponata variations. This traditional dish, a tasty mix of vegetables with a sweet-and-sour dressing, was often a one-course meal for the lower classes, sometimes accompanied by a chunk of bread. Some scholars say that the term caponata comes from the aristocratic custom of eating this colorful salad as a side dish with a fish called pesce cappone (tub gurnard). Others believe that it refers to the cauponae, lively taverns frequented by sailors. The dishes may have been "poor," but they were rich with flavor and aroma.

MEDITERRANEAN-STYLE TOMATOES

POMODORI ALLA MEDITERRANEA

Preparation time: 20 minutes + 15 minutes cooking time

4 Servings

1 lb. 2 oz. (500 g) **tomatoes**
Salt to taste
1 tsp. **finely chopped fresh parsley**
1 tsp. **finely chopped fresh basil**
1/2 tsp. **fresh thyme leaves**
1/2 tsp. **fresh oregano leaves**
1/2 tsp. **fresh marjoram leaves**
1 1/4 cups (125 g) **plain breadcrumbs**
1/4 cup (60 ml) **extra-virgin olive oil**

Method

Heat the oven to 350°F (175°C).

Stem and halve the tomatoes. Place them in a colander, sprinkle with salt, and let them drain for about 15 minutes.

Meanwhile, finely chop together the herbs, then place them in a bowl. Add the breadcrumbs and the olive oil, and mix well.

Spread the breadcrumb mixture over the cut side of the tomato halves and arrange them in a baking pan. Bake for about 15 minutes, or until the breadcrumbs are golden-brown.

A beneficial herb

Thyme (scientific name Thymus vulgaris*) is a small bush with green-grey leaves which give off an intense aroma. It is rich in vitamins C and B and mineral salts such as manganese, iron, potassium, calcium, and magnesium. Thyme also has medicinal properties and has been used as a balm, an antiseptic, an aid to digestion, an antioxidant, a diuretic, antibiotic, painkiller and to strengthen the immune system. In cooking, it is used as an aromatic herb as well as an ingredient in preserving food and in creating brine, as it prevents the formation of mold.*

Difficulty

FAVA BEAN FRITTERS
PANELLE DI FAVE

Preparation time: 5 minutes + overnight soaking + 3 1/2 hours cooking time

4 Servings

2 1/4 lbs. (1 kg) **dried fava beans**
Salt to taste
1 **small yellow onion, cut into**
  1/2-inch-thick slices
2 to 3 **fennel fronds (preferably wild)**
Extra-virgin olive oil
Vegetable oil for frying
Crushed red pepper flakes (optional)

Method

Place the fava beans in a large bowl of cold water to cover by 2 inches and soak overnight.

Drain and rinse the beans, then place in a large saucepan. Add the onion, fennel, and cold water to cover by 2 inches. Bring to a boil, then reduce to a simmer. Cook, adding water if necessary to keep the beans covered, until the beans have softened into a purée, 2 to 3 hours.

Remove and discard the onion and fennel. Strain the purée through a medium-mesh seive to extract excess liquid.

Place the purée on a well-oiled work surface or a rimmed baking sheet. Shape the mixture into a 1-inch (3 cm) thick rectangle. Allow to cool, then cut into strips about 2 inches (5 cm) long and 10 inches (25 cm) wide.

Heat 1/2 inch of vegetable oil in a large skillet over medium-high heat until shimmering. Fry the fritters until golden-brown on all sides. Using a slotted spoon, transfer the fritters to paper towels to drain. Sprinkle with salt and crushed red pepper to taste, if desired. Serve hot.

Difficulty

POTATO POLENTA
POLENTA DI PATATE

Preparation time: 15 minutes +1 hour cooking time

4 to 6 Servings

6 1/3 cups (1 1/2 l) **water**
2 1/2 tbsp. (35 g) **unsalted butter**
1 lb. (500 g) **potatoes, peeled and cut
    into 1/2-inch cubes (1 cm)**
Salt to taste
1 1/2 cups (250 g) **cornmeal**
**Grated Parmigiano Reggiano or
    Pecorino cheese (optional)**

Method

Bring the water to a boil with the butter in a large saucepan. Add the potatoes and 3/4 teaspoon salt. Cook until the potatoes are tender and easily pierced with the tip of a paring knife, 10 to 15 minutes. Whisk in the cornmeal. Reduce the heat to low and cook, stirring constantly with a wooden spoon, until the polenta is tender, about 40 minutes.

Adjust the seasoning to taste. Serve immediately, sprinkled with the cheese, if desired.

Difficulty

Chef's Tip

Any leftover polenta can be chilled for up to 3 days. Before serving, slice and warm through in the oven, on the grill, or in a skillet with butter or olive oil.

BAKED FENNEL

FINOCCHI ALLA PARMIGIANA

Preparation time: 10 minutes + 20 minutes cooking time

4 Servings

Salt and freshly ground black pepper
   to taste
14 oz. (400 g) **fennel bulbs, stalks and
   fronds removed**
3 1/2 tbsp. (50 g) **unsalted butter**
3 oz. (100 g) **Parmigiano Reggiano
   cheese, grated**

Method

Heat the oven to 375°F (190°C).

Bring a large pot of salted water to a boil and cook the fennel until crisp-tender, about 15 minutes; drain.

Let the fennel cool, then cut it in half lengthwise. Cut out and discard the core, then cut the bulb lenthwise into thick slices.

Butter a 2-quart baking dish. Melt the remaining butter in a saucepan. In the baking dish, arrange a layer of fennel, then sprinkle with some of the Parmigiano and drizzle with some melted butter. Add a second layer of fennel and continue in the same manner until all the ingredients are used.

Bake until the top is browned, about 10 minutes. Serve sprinkled with pepper.

Difficulty

VEGETABLE STACKS
MILLEFOGLIE VEGETARIANO

Preparation time: 30 minutes + cooking time: 55 minutes + 15 minutes marinating time

4 Servings

7 oz. (200 g) **leeks, white parts only**

1/3 cup (100 ml) **whole milk**

All-purpose flour

Vegetable oil for frying

Salt and freshly ground black pepper to taste

7 oz. (200 g) **yellow bell peppers (about 2 medium)**

6 **small Italian eggplants, cut crosswise into 1/8-inch (3 mm) thick rounds**

9 oz. (250 g) **large zucchini, cut crosswise into 1/8-inch (3 mm) thick rounds**

7 oz. (200 g) **red onion, peeled and cut crosswise into 1/8-inch (3 mm) thick rounds**

7 oz. (200 g) **yellow summer squash, cut into 1/8-inch (3 mm) thick rounds**

7 oz. (200 g) **fennel bulb, cut lengthwise through the core into 1/8-inch (3 mm) thick slices**

5 oz. (150 g) **small heads radicchio, cut lengthwise through the core into 1/8-inch (3 mm) thick slices**

Juice from 1 lemon

5 oz. (150 g) **celery root, peeled and cut crosswise into 1/8-inch (3 mm) thick rounds**

10 oz. (300 g) **large tomatoes (about 2), cut crosswise into 1/8-inch (3 mm) thick rounds**

3 1/2 tbsp. (50 ml) **extra-virgin olive oil plus more for drizzling**

Difficulty

Method

Cut the leeks lengthwise into thin strips. Soak for 10 minutes in the milk, then drain. Dredge the leeks in flour.

Heat 1/2 inch of vegetable oil in a medium frying pan over medium-high heat until shimmering. Fry the leeks until crispy. Using a slotted spoon, transfer the leeks to paper towels to drain. Season with salt and set aside.

Heat the oven to 475°F (245°C).

Roast or grill the bell peppers (directly over the flame on a grill or stovetop), then transfer to a medium bowl, cover with plastic wrap, and let sit for 10 to 15 minutes. Peel the peppers, remove and discard the seeds, and slice them crosswise into rounds.

Arrange the eggplant, zucchini, onion, squash, fennel, and radicchio in a single layer on 2 or 3 baking sheets. Drizzle with a few drops of oil. Roast until tender, about 35 minutes.

Bring a medium pot of salted water to a boil. Add a few drops of lemon juice to the boiling water and cook the celery root for 5 minutes.

Place all the cooked vegetables and the tomatoes in a large bowl, season with salt and pepper, drizzle with olive oil, and let marinate for at least 15 minutes.

Layer the vegetables to create stacks. Garnish with the fried leeks.

RÖSTI

RÖSTI

Preparation time: 10 minutes + 20 minutes cooking time

4 Servings

1 3/4 lbs. (750 g) **potatoes, peeled**
3 1/2 tbsp. (50 g) **unsalted butter**
Salt and freshly ground black pepper

Method

On the large holes of a box grater, grate the potatoes. Squeeze out as much liquid as possible.

Melt the butter in a large nonstick skillet over medium-low heat and add the potatoes. Season with salt and pepper and stir using two spatulas.

When the potatoes begin to soften, flatten them using the spatulas, shaping them into pancake form. Continue to cook until the bottom is crispy and golden, 12 to 15 minutes.

Invert onto a plate, then slide back into the skillet, browned side up. Cook until the second side is golden-brown and the center is tender. Serve immediately.

Difficulty

RATATOUILLE

RATATUIA

Preparation time: 10 minutes + 20 minutes cooking time

4 Servings

1/3 cup plus 2 tbsp. (100 ml) **extra-virgin olive oil**

6 1/3 oz. (180 g) **onions (about 2 1/2 small)**

1 **garlic clove**

3 1/2 oz. (100 g) **red bell peppers (about 2 1/2 small), cut into 3/4-inch (2 cm) cubes**

3 1/2 oz. (100 g) **yellow bell peppers (about 1 1/2 small), cut into 3/4-inch (2 cm) cubes**

7 oz. (200 g) **eggplant (about 1/3 medium), cut into 3/4-inch (2 cm) cubes**

10 1/2 oz. (300 g) **zucchini (about 1 1/2 medium), cut into 3/4-inch (2 cm) cubes**

7 oz. (200 g) **tomatoes (about 1 1/2 medium), cut into 3/4-inch (2 cm) cubes**

Salt and freshly ground black pepper to taste

4 **large fresh basil leaves, torn into pieces, plus whole leaves for garnish**

Difficulty

Method

Heat the oil, onion, and whole garlic clove in a large skillet over medium. Cook until softened, then add the red and yellow bell peppers. After a few minutes add the eggplant, then the zucchini. Cook for 3 to 4 minutes, then add the tomatoes and a generous pinch of salt and pepper.

Reduce the heat to low and cook, stirring occasionally, until the tomatoes are falling apart and the flavors have blended, then stir in the basil. Adjust the seasoning to taste.

Serve garnished with whole basil leaves.

Vegetables in Mediterranean culture

The ubiquity of vegetables is undoubtedly the element that most inspired Doctor Ancel Keys and his colleagues to outline the nutritional and dietary model known as the "Mediterranean diet." The use of herbs and vegetables of every kind has always been a well-known trait of Italian cooking. One need only consider that Liber de coquina, which dates to the 13th or perhaps even the 12th century, begins with a series of recipes for vegetables. And after all, cabbage, spinach, fennel, and herbs have always been featured players in Italian culinary history.

BUTTERNUT SQUASH GRATIN

ZUCCA GRATINATA

Preparation time: 20 minutes + 35 minutes cooking time

4 Servings

1 lb. 11 oz. (750 g) **butternut squash**
3/4 cup (150 ml) **heavy cream**
1 cup (200 ml) **whole milk**
Salt and freshly ground white pepper
Unsalted butter for greasing the pan

Method

Heat the oven to 350°F (175°C).

Peel the squash, then cut it in half lengthwise. Scoop out and discard the seeds. Cut the flesh crosswise into 1/8-inch (3 mm) thick slices.

Place the cream in a large saucepan. Add the squash, then the milk and a generous pinch of salt and white pepper. Cover and cook over medium heat until the squash is tender.

Grease a 10-inch (25 cm) round baking dish and arrange the slices of squash in layers in it. Bake for about 20 minutes, until the top is golden in spots. Let cool completely on a wire rack.

Use a knife to cut the gratin into shapes (as pictured), if desired. Before serving, warm in the oven at 350°F (175°C) for a few minutes.

Difficulty

BROCCOLI RAAB WITH GARLIC AND OIL

CIME DI RAPA SALTATE

Preparation time: 5 minutes + 15 minutes cooking time

4 Servings

3 1/2 tbsp. (50 ml) **extra-virgin olive oil**

2 **cloves garlic, thinly sliced**

Crushed red pepper flakes to taste

3 1/3 lbs. (1.5 kg) **broccoli raab, chopped**

Salt to taste

Method

Heat the olive oil with the garlic and the crushed red pepper in a large skillet over medium-low heat until the garlic is lightly golden but not browned.

Add the broccoli raab.

Season with salt, increase the heat to medium, and cook, stirring frequently, until the broccoli raab is tender, about 10 minutes.

Serve immediately.

Vegetable gardens

Since antiquity, vegetable gardens have played a fundamental role in Mediterranean cuisine, so much so that even today almost every Italian country house has its own garden to draw from when seasonal produce is needed. The vegetable garden first acquired some prestige in conjunction with the monastic culture of the High Middle Ages. Various authors refer to them as a prefiguration of heaven on earth. Christianity is undoubtedly the origin of this enhanced sensibility, more spiritual and poetic than gastronomic regarding products of the earth. The Italian landscape is decorated with vegetable gardens. But what did the earth have to offer to the medieval table? At that time, gardens contained ornamental (some edible), medicinal, and alimentary plants. The latter includes cucumbers, melon, pumpkin, chard, spinach, onions, leeks, radishes, peas, and – above all – cabbage, the undisputed king of the poor and humble kitchen. Herbs were also widely cultivated throughout the Italian peninsula, and their unmistakable fragrances helped to distinguish Italian cuisine from the rest of European cuisine.

Difficulty

FRIED POLENTA

SCAGLIOZZI

Preparation time: 50 minutes cooking time

4 Servings

2 cups (1/2 l) **water**
3/4 cup **cornmeal**
Olive oil for frying
Salt to taste

Method

Bring the water to a boil in a medium pot (use a copper pot if possible).

Pour the cornmeal into the boiling water in a slow, steady stream, whisking constantly. Cook over low heat until thickened, about 30 minutes, stirring frequently with a wooden spoon.

Pour the polenta into a greased baking pan. Spread it to a thickness of about 1/2 inch (1 cm) and let it cool completely. Cut the cooled polenta into 1-inch (3 cm) thick slices.

Heat 1/2 inch of oil in a large nonstick skillet until shimmering. Fry the polenta slices until golden-brown and crisp, about 8 minutes per side. Using a slotted spoon, transfer the polenta to paper towels to drain. Sprinkle with salt to taste and serve very hot.

Difficulty

PIZZA & FOCACCIA

CHAPTER SIX

PIZZA WITH ARUGULA AND PARMIGIANO REGGIANO
PIZZA CON RUCOLA E PARMIGIANO REGGIANO

Preparation time: 15 minutes + 2 to 7 hours rising time + 20 minutes cooking time

4 Servings

FOR THE DOUGH

4 cups (500 g) **all-purpose flour**
1 1/2 cups (350 ml) **lukewarm water**
1 or 2 tsp. (4 g or 8 g) **active dry yeast (see method per amount of yeast)**
1 1/2 tbsp. (20 ml) **extra-virgin olive oil, plus more for greasing**
1/5 oz. (4 g) **salt**

FOR THE TOPPING

14 1/2-oz. (400 g) **can whole peeled tomatoes, drained and coarsely chopped**
14 oz. (400 g) **fresh mozzarella, shredded and at room temperature**
3 1/2 oz. (100 g) **baby arugula**
5 1/4 oz. (150 g) **Parmigiano Reggiano cheese, shaved**

Method

Make the dough: Make a well in the flour on a pastry board. Pour in the water, into which the yeast has been dissolved, and begin kneading. Add the oil and finally the salt. Continue working the dough until it is soft, smooth, and elastic.

Grease the dough with oil, transfer to a bowl, cover it with plastic wrap, and let rest at warm room temperature for 10 minutes. Then gently lay it out on an oil-greased baking sheet. Imagine you are playing the piano and, using only your fingertips, stretch the dough out into a round to fit the baking sheet.

Let the dough rise for 40 minutes if you have used 2 teaspoons of yeast. If you have used 1 teaspoon, place the baking sheet, covered with plastic wrap, in the refrigerator for at least 5 to 6 hours. The dough will rise perfectly well in the refrigerator and be light and aromatic.

After it rises, spread the peeled tomatoes and mozzarella over the pizza.

Once you have garnished the pizza, let it rise at warm room temperature for another 40 minutes or so. Meanwhile, heat the oven to 425°F (220°C).

Bake the pizza for about 20 minutes, or until the cheese is bubbly and the crust is golden-brown. Serve garnished with the arugula and shaved Parmigiano Reggiano.

Difficulty

PIZZA WITH EGG
PIZZA ALL'UOVO

Preparation time: 30 minutes + 1 1/2 to 2 hours rising time + 8 minutes cooking time

4 Servings

FOR THE DOUGH
5 cups (650 g) **all-purpose flour**
1 1/2 tsp. (2 g) **active dry yeast**
1 1/2 cups (375 ml) **lukewarm water**
1 tbsp. (18 g) **salt**
Extra-virgin olive oil for greasing

FOR THE TOPPING
3/4 28-oz. can (600 g) **crushed tomatoes**
Salt to taste
Dried oregano
Extra-virgin olive oil
1 lb. 2 oz. (500 g) **fresh mozzarella, thinly sliced**
4 **large eggs**

Method

Make the dough: Put the flour onto a clean work surface and make a well in the center. Dissolve the yeast in the water, and pour into the well. Gradually incorporate into the flour until a loose dough forms; add the salt. Knead the dough until smooth. Transfer to a bowl, cover with lightly oiled plastic wrap, and let rise until doubled in volume, about 1 hour.

Divide the dough into 4 portions and roll them into balls. Cover with a clean kitchen towel. Let them rise again until they have again doubled in size (from 30 minutes to 1 hour, depending on the ambient temperature).

Make the topping: Season the tomatoes with salt to taste, a pinch of oregano, and a little drizzle of oil.

Dust a work surface with flour and flatten each dough ball, starting with your fingertips and progressing to a rotary movement of your hands as the dough gets flatter and wider, into a 1/3-inch (1 cm) thick round. Put the dough rounds on a baking sheet.

Heat the oven to 475°F (245°C). Spread the crushed tomatoes over the dough rounds and top with mozzarella. Crack an egg onto the middle of each pizza. Bake for 7 to 8 minutes, or until the cheese is bubbly and the crust is golden-brown.

Difficulty

TOMATO, OLIVE, AND RICOTTA SALATA CALZONES
CALZONE BARESE

Preparation time: 10 minutes + 1 hour rising time + 20 minutes cooking time

4 Servings

FOR THE DOUGH

4 cups (500 g) all-purpose flour or
  Italian "00" flour, plus more as
  needed
3/4 tsp. (2 g) active dry yeast
1/2 cup (125 ml) lukewarm water
1/2 cup (100 ml) extra-virgin olive oil
Salt

FOR THE TOPPING

1 lb. (500 g) ripe tomatoes (about
  5 medium)
3 1/2 tbsp. (50 ml) extra-virgin olive
  oil
1 small onion, thinly sliced
Salt and freshly ground black pepper
3 1/2 oz. (100 g) black olives, pitted
  and finely chopped
5 oz. (150 g) ricotta salata

Method

Make the dough: Put the flour on a clean work surface; make a well in the center. Dissolve the yeast in the water, then pour it into the well. Add the oil to the well. Gradually incorporate into the flour until a loose dough forms; add a pinch of salt. Knead the dough until it is smooth. Form the dough into 4 balls. Cover with a clean dishtowel and let rise at warm room temperature for 1 hour.

Make the filling: Prepare the tomatoes by making an X-shaped incision on the bottom of each tomato and blanching them in boiling water for 10 to 15 seconds. Immediately submerge the tomatoes in ice water for 1 to 2 minutes, then peel, seed, and coarsely chop.

In a medium pan, heat the oil over medium. Sauté the onion until it is soft and translucent. Add the tomatoes. Cook until the mixture thickens, about 5 minutes. Add the olives, then stir in the ricotta. Season with salt and pepper to taste. Remove from the heat.

Heat the oven to 475°F (245°C).

On a floured work surface, flatten each dough ball, starting with your fingertips and progressing to a rotary movement of your hands as the dough gets flatter and wider, into a round about 8 inches in diameter. Put the rounds on a lightly oiled baking sheet. Divide the filling among the rounds, spreading it over half of each round, then fold the dough in half and seal the edges.

Bake the calzones for about 20 minutes, or until the crust is golden-brown.

Difficulty

SPINACH PIE

ERBAZZONE

Preparation time: 1 hour + 30 minutes cooking time

4 Servings

FOR THE DOUGH

1 cup (150 g) **all-purpose flour**
3/4 tsp. (5 g) **salt**
1 tbsp. (15 g) **cold unsalted butter**
Sparkling water, as needed
Extra-virgin olive oil for greasing

FOR THE FILLING

1 1/2 oz. (40 g) **vegetable shortening**
1 lb. (453 g) **chard, chopped**
3/4 lb. (340 g) **spinach, chopped**
2/3 cup (100 g) **onion, finely chopped**
1 **clove garlic, finely chopped**
Salt to taste
Ground nutmeg to taste
1 3/4 oz. (50 g) **Parmigiano Reggiano
  cheese, grated**
Plain breadcrumbs, as needed
**Extra-virgin olive oil for greasing the
  pan**

Method

Make the dough: Whisk together the flour and salt. Cut the butter into the flour until the texture is pebbly. Add sparkling water as needed, just until the dough begins to form.

Turn the dough out onto a floured work surface and knead until it is smooth. Let the dough rest, loosely covered with lightly oiled plastic wrap, for 10 minutes.

Make the filling: Heat the oven to 400°F (200°C). Heat three-quarters of the shortening in a large skillet over medium. Sauté the chard and spinach until wilted.

Add the onion and garlic, and sauté. Add a pinch of salt and nutmeg, the Parmigiano, and enough breadcrumbs to form a firm filling.

Divide the dough into 2 balls, one slightly larger. Roll out the larger ball to a 1/8-inch-thick square, line a lightly oiled baking pan with the dough. Spread with the filling. Roll out the second ball to a 1/8-inch-thick square. Place on top of the filling, then pinch the edges to seal.

Dot the top with the remaining shortening, then pierce the dough all over with a fork. Bake in the oven for about 30 minutes, or until the top is golden.

Difficulty

SUN-DRIED TOMATO AND CAPER LOAF

CAKE AI POMODORI SECCHI

Preparation time: 15 minutes + 40 minutes cooking time

4 Servings

3 **large eggs**

2 tbsp. (30 ml) **extra-virgin olive oil**

1/3 cup plus 1 1/2 tbsp. (100 ml) **whole milk**

Salt and freshly ground black pepper to taste

1 2/3 cups (200 g) **all-purpose flour, plus more for dusting**

1/4 oz. (7 g) **active dry yeast**

1 cup (100 g) **freshly grated Pecorino cheese**

3 1/2 oz. (100 g) **sun-dried tomatoes**

3 tbsp. (25 g) **capers, rinsed, drained and coarsely chopped**

1 tbsp. (5 g) **fresh oregano, finely chopped**

Unsalted butter and all-purpose flour for pan

Method

Heat the oven to 350°F (175°C).

Beat the eggs with the oil and milk in a large bowl, then season with a pinch of salt and pepper.

Add the flour and yeast and mix well. Stir in the Pecorino, sun-dried tomatoes, capers, and oregano.

Butter a loaf pan, dust it with flour, and fill it with the batter (the pan should be about three-quarters full).

Bake for 35 to 40 minutes, or until a toothpick inserted in the center comes out clean.

Set the pan on a wire rack to cool for 5 minutes, then turn the loaf out onto the rack and let cool completely.

Difficulty

FOCACCIA WITH OLIVES AND ROBIOLA CHEESE
FOCACCIA ALLE OLIVE CON ROBIOLA

Preparation time: 25 minutes + 1 1/2 hours rising time + 25 minutes cooking time

4 Servings

FOR THE DOUGH

4 cups (500 g) **all-purpose flour**
1 1/2 tsp. (4 g) **active dry yeast**
1 cup plus 2 tbsp. (270 ml) **lukewarm water**
1 tbsp. (10 g) **diastatic malt powder or 1/2 tbsp. (10 g) honey**
2 tbsp. plus 2 tsp. (40 ml) **extra-virgin olive oil, plus more for greasing**
1 1/2 tsp. (10 g) **salt**

FOR THE BRINE

1/2 cup (100 ml) **water**
3 tbsp plus 1 tsp. (50 ml) **extra-virgin olive oil**
2 1/4 tsp. (14 g) **coarse salt**

FOR THE FILLING AND GARNISH

1/2 cup (100 g) **pitted olives**
1 1/4 cups (300 g) **fresh Robiola cheese, at room temperature**

Method

Make the dough: Put the flour onto a clean work surface; make a well in the center. Dissolve the yeast in the lukewarm water. Pour it into the mixture, then add the honey into the well. Gradually incorporate them into the flour. Add the oil and salt. Knead the dough until smooth. Cover with oiled plastic wrap; let rise at warm room temperature for 30 minutes.

Make the brine: Combine the water, olive oil, and coarse salt in a bowl. Stir to make an emulsion. Let it rest for a few minutes.

Assemble the focaccia: Grease a large rimmed baking sheet. Place the dough on the baking sheet, and stretch it gently with your fingertips to form a rectangle slightly smaller than the sheet. Prod the dough surface with your fingers, forming dimples where the seasoning will collect. Drizzle the focaccia with the brine, then let it rise at warm room temperature, uncovered, until doubled in volume, about 1 hour.

Heat the oven to 400°F (200°C). Scatter the olives on the focaccia. Bake for 25 minutes, or until golden brown. Remove from oven and let cool.

Using a bread knife, cut the cooled focaccia into individual rectangles and then cut them in half lengthwise. Soften the Robiola cheese by stirring it with a dash of oil. Spread, then sandwich it between the focaccia halves to form sandwiches.

Difficulty

EASTER CHEESE BREAD
TORTA DI PASQUA AL FORMAGGIO

Preparation time: 1 hour 30 minutes + 40 minutes cooking time

4 Servings

4 eggs (1 for the egg wash)
1 cup plus 3 tbsp. (120 g) freshly
  grated Pecorino cheese
Salt and freshly ground black pepper
  to taste
1 3/4 tsp. (11 g) active dry yeast
1/3 cup plus 1 1/2 tbsp. (100 ml)
  lukewarm water
5 1/2 tbsp. (75 g) unsalted butter, plus
  more for greasing
2 2/3 cups (325 g) all-purpose flour
1 1/2 tsp. (7 g) baking powder
1/3 cup plus 2 1/2 tbsp. (50 g)
  breadcrumbs

Method

Beat 3 of the eggs with the 1 cup of grated Pecorino cheese and a pinch of salt and pepper. Dissolve the yeast in the lukewarm water. Pour it into the mixture, then add the butter and mix in the flour and baking powder.

Grease four popover molds with butter, then dust with the breadcrumbs. Fill them halfway with dough. Let the dough rise at warm room temperature until it doubles in bulk.

Heat the oven to 350°F (175°C).

Beat the remaining egg. Brush the tops of the dough with it. Sprinkle the dough with freshly ground pepper and the remaining 3 tablespoons of grated Pecorino. Bake for about 40 minutes.

Ritual foods

The millennial culture of food has always been closely tied to the agricultural calendar and religious liturgy. In the Italian Catholic tradition, Easter is definitely the most important holiday of the year. Anthropologically speaking, rituality entered the domestic environment mainly through food. Eating habits punctuate the rhythms of the year and of life, and transmit archetypical symbols to the community.

Eggs are clearly the predominant symbol and food item for Easter celebrations. A universal sign of genesis and rebirth – perhaps because it's considered the equivalent of a primordial seed that's complete in and of itself – the egg conveys a sense of both fully formed life and potential life.

Over time the value of the egg has changed, but it hasn't lost the centrality it's always enjoyed as a symbol of Easter. Today it represents prosperity, joy, and renewal in general, beyond any religious affiliations.

Difficulty

CHICKPEA FOCACCIA
FOCACCIA DI CECI

Preparation time: 30 minutes + 2 hours rising time + 20 minutes cooking time

4 Servings

FOR THE DOUGH

3 cups (375 g) **all-purpose flour or cake flour**
1 1/3 cups (125 g) **chickpea flour**
1 1/2 tsp. (10 g) **salt**
1 2/3 cups (280 ml) **lukewarm water**
1 tbsp. (8 g) **active dry yeast**
1 tbsp. (10 g) **diastatic malt powder**
2 1/4 tsp. (10 ml) **extra-virgin olive oil**

FOR THE TOPPING

3 1/2 tbsp. (50 ml) **extra-virgin olive oil**
Coarsely ground black pepper to taste

Method

Make the dough: Mix together the two types of flour on a clean work surface and make a well in the center. Dissolve the salt in 3 tablespoons of the lukewarm water. Dissolve the yeast in the remaining water.

Pour the yeast mixture into the well, and gradually start incorporating it into the flour. Add the malt and the oil and, lastly, the salt mixture. Knead the dough until soft, smooth, and elastic.

Loosely cover the dough with a sheet of lightly oiled plastic wrap and let rise at warm room temperature until it has doubled in volume (about 1 hour).

Assemble the focaccia: Divide the dough into 4 balls. Place them in a lightly oiled baking pan and let rise at warm room temperature for about 30 minutes.

Flatten the dough into disks. Prod the surface of the dough with your fingers, forming small dimples where the seasoning will collect. Brush the surface with the oil and sprinkle with fresh coarsely ground pepper. Let the focaccia rise for another 30 minutes.

Heat the oven to 425°F (220°C). Bake for about 20 minutes, or until golden-brown.

Difficulty

APULIAN-STYLE PIZZA
PIZZA PUGLIESE

Preparation time: 15 minutes + 1 1/2 hours rising time + 20 minutes cooking time

4 Servings

FOR THE DOUGH

4 cups (500 g) all-purpose flour or Italian "00" flour, plus more as needed

1 1/2 tsp. (4 g) active dry yeast

1 1/2 cups (350 ml) lukewarm water

1 1/2 tbsp. (20 ml) extra-virgin olive oil, plus more for greasing the pan

2 tsp. (12 g) salt

FOR THE TOPPING

14 1/2 oz. (200 g) can whole peeled tomatoes, juices drained, tomatoes crushed by hand

7 slices Caciocavallo or provolone cheese

2 medium yellow onions, sliced into 1/4-inch-thick (1/2 cm) rounds

10 green and black olives, pitted and sliced

Dried oregano (optional)

Method

Make the dough: Put the flour onto a clean work surface and make a well in the center. Dissolve the yeast in the water, and pour the yeast mixture into the well. Gradually start incorporating the yeast mixture into the flour until a loose dough starts to form, then add the oil and salt.

Knead the dough until smooth and elastic. Rub the dough with a little oil, loosely cover with plastic wrap, and let it rest for about 10 minutes.

Oil a 12-inch round pizza pan. Transfer the dough to the pan and, using your fingertips, spread the dough to cover the bottom of the pan.

Let the dough rise at warm room temperature for 40 minutes.

Assemble the pizza: Top the dough with the tomatoes, cheese, onions, and olives (all at room temperature). Let it rise for 40 minutes more.

Heat the oven to 425°F (220°C).

Bake the pizza for 20 minutes, or until the cheese is bubbly and the crust is golden-brown. Garnish with oregano, if desired.

Difficulty

CRESCIONE WITH BEET GREENS

CRESCIONE ALLE ERBETTE

Preparation time: 30 minutes + 1 hour rising time + 8 minutes cooking time

4 Servings

FOR THE DOUGH

4 cups (500 g) **all-purpose flour or cake flour**

1/2 cup (125 ml) **lukewarm whole milk**

1 **large egg**

1 tbsp. (15 g) **baking powder**

3 oz. (75 g) **vegetable shortening, softened**

1 2/3 tsp. (10 g) **salt**

FOR THE FILLING

1 lb. (500 g) **beet greens**

1 oz. (25 g) **vegetable shortening, softened, or olive oil**

1 **clove garlic, peeled**

Salt and freshly ground black pepper

1 oz. (30 g) **Parmigiano Reggiano cheese**

1 tbsp. plus 2 tsp. (25 ml) **extra-virgin olive oil**

Method

Make the dough: Put the flour on a clean work surface and make a well in the center. Add the milk, egg, baking powder, shortening, and salt to the well; mix the wet ingredients to blend. Gradually blend into the flour, and begin to knead. Continue kneading the dough until it is smooth and elastic.

Cover the dough with a kitchen towel and let it rest at warm room temperature for at least 1 hour.

Make the filling: Thoroughly rinse and drain the beet greens. In a large pot, heat the shortening over medium and sauté the beet greens and the whole clove of garlic. Add a pinch of salt and pepper. Cook for 5 minutes. Discard the garlic. Let the greens cool, then chop them coarsely. Mix in the Parmigiano.

Divide the dough into 4 small loaves. Roll them out into discs 1/8 inch (3 mm) thick and 10 to 12 inches (25 to 30 cm) in diameter. Put some of the cooked greens in the middle of each disc, fold in half and seal the edges.

Brush the oil on top of the crescione, then cook on a greased griddle or in a large nonstick skillet over high heat for 4 minutes on each side, or until they are golden-brown and warmed through.

Difficulty

PIZZA WITH EGGPLANT AND PROVOLA CHEESE

PIZZA MELANZANA, PROVOLA, E PACHINO

Preparation time: 30 minutes + 1 hour rising time + 15 minutes cooking time

4 Servings

FOR THE DOUGH

5 cups (650 g) **all-purpose flour or Italian "00" flour, plus more as needed**

1 1/2 tsp. (2 g) **active dry yeast**

1 1/2 cups plus 1 tsp. (375 ml) **lukewarm water**

1 tbsp. (18 g) **salt**

FOR THE TOPPING

1 lb. (500 g) **crushed tomatoes**

Salt to taste

Extra-virgin olive oil

11 oz. (300 g) **eggplant**

1 lb. (500 g) **Sicilian Provola, or Fontina or Pecorino cheese, thinly sliced**

9 oz. (250 g) **Pachino or cherry tomatoes, stemmed and cut crosswise in half**

Method

Make the dough: Put the flour on a clean work surface and make a well in the center. Dissolve the yeast in the water and pour it into the well. Gradually incorporate it into the flour until a loose dough forms, then add the salt. Knead the dough until smooth and elastic. Loosely cover the dough with lightly oiled plastic wrap and let it rise until it doubles in volume, about 1 hour.

Make the filling: Season the crushed tomatoes with salt and a little drizzle of olive oil. Slice and grill the eggplant, or fry the slices in olive oil, then drain.

Heat the oven to 475°F (245°C).

Dust a work surface with flour and flatten each dough ball, starting with your fingertips and progressing to a rotary movement of your hands as the dough gets flatter and wider, into a round about 8 inches in diameter. Put the rounds on a baking sheet.

Spread the crushed tomatoes over the pizzas and top with the cheese, tomatoes, and eggplant. Bake for 8 minutes, or until the cheese is bubbly and the crust is golden-brown.

Difficulty

ONION FOCACCIA
FOCACCIA ALLE CIPOLLE

Preparation time: 20 minutes + 1 1/2 hours rising time + 20 minutes cooking time

4 Servings

FOR THE FOCACCIA

4 cups (500 g) **all-purpose flour**

2 1/2 tsp. (10 g) **sugar**

1 1/2 tsp. (4.5 g) **active dry yeast**

1 cup plus 2 tbsp. (270 ml) **lukewarm water**

2 tbsp. plus 2 tsp. (40 ml) **extra-virgin olive oil**

1 1/2 tsp. (10 g) **salt**

FOR THE BRINE

1 2/3 tbsp. (25 ml) **water**

3 tbsp. (45 ml) **extra-virgin olive oil**

2 tsp. (7 g) **coarse salt**

FOR THE TOPPING

12 oz. (350 g) **onions, thinly sliced**

Method

Put the flour onto a clean work surface, make a well in the center, and add the sugar. Dissolve the yeast in the lukewarm water. Pour the yeast mixture into the well, and gradually start incorporating it into the flour a little at a time. Add the oil and then the salt. Knead the dough until soft, smooth, and elastic.

Loosely cover the dough with a sheet of lightly greased plastic wrap and let rise in a warm place for about 30 minutes.

To make the brine, combine the water, olive oil, and coarse salt in a bowl. Stir to make an emulsion and then let it rest.

Transfer the dough to a lightly oiled baking pan, stretching it gently with your fingertips. Prod the surface of the dough with your fingers, forming small dimples where the seasoning will collect. Sprinkle the focaccia with the brine, then let the dough rise until it has doubled in volume, about 1 hour.

Heat the oven to 400°F (205°C).

In a large skillet, sauté the onions in a little olive oil until softened. Remove the pan from the heat, and spread the onions over the focaccia. Bake for 20 minutes, or until golden-brown.

Difficulty

FOCACCIA FROM NOVI LIGURE

FOCACCIA NOVESE O DI NOVI LIGURE

Preparation time: 15 minutes + 1 1/2 hours rising time + 20 minutes cooking time

4 Servings

FOR THE FOCACCIA

4 cups (500 g) **all-purpose flour**
1 1/2 tsp. (4 1/4 g) **active dry yeast**
1 cup plus 1 tbsp. plus 2 tsp. (275 ml)
  lukewarm water
1 1/2 tsp. (5 g) **diastatic malt powder
  or 3/4 tsp. (5 g) honey**
1 tbsp. plus 2 tsp. (20 g) **softened
  vegetable shortening**
1 tbsp. plus 2 tsp. (25 ml) **extra-virgin
  olive oil**
1 1/2 tsp. (10 g) **salt**

FOR THE GENOESE BRINE

1/2 cup (100 ml) **water**
3 tbsp. plus 2 tsp. (50 ml) **extra-virgin
  olive oil**
2 tsp. (14 g) **coarse salt**

Method

Put the flour onto a clean work surface and make a well in the center. Dissolve the yeast in the lukewarm water. Pour the yeast mixture and malt into the well, and gradually start incorporating them into the flour a little at a time. Stir in the shortening and the oil then add the salt. Knead the dough until soft, smooth, and elastic.

Loosely cover the dough with a sheet of lightly oiled plastic wrap and let the dough rise at warm room temperature for about 1 hour.

To make the brine, combine the water, olive oil, and coarse salt in a bowl. Stir to make an emulsion and then let it rest.

Transfer the dough to a lightly oiled baking pan, stretching it gently with your fingertips until 1/2 inch (1 cm) thick. Prod the surface of the dough with your fingers, forming small dimples where the seasoning will collect. Sprinkle the focaccia with the brine, then let the dough rise until doubled in volume, about 30 minutes.

Heat the oven to 450°F (230°C).

Bake the foccacia for 20 minutes, or until golden-brown. Remove the focaccia from the oven and, while hot, brush with olive oil.

Difficulty

PUMPKIN BREAD

PANE ALLA ZUCCA

Preparation time: 1 hour + 1 hour and 10 minutes rising time + 45 minutes cooking

4 to 6 Servings

5 1/4 oz. (150 g) **butternut squash**
4 cups (500 g) **all-purpose flour**
2 tbsp. (12 g) **active dry yeast**
1 cup (225 ml) **lukewarm water**
1 1/2 tbsp. (20 ml) **extra-virgin olive oil**
2 tsp. (13 g) **salt**

Method

Heat the oven to 350°F (175°C).

Peel and seed the squash and cut into 3- or 4-inch (8-10 cm) cubes. Wrap the pieces in aluminum foil, place on a baking sheet, and bake until tender, about 20 minutes. Once cooked, let cool.

Put the flour onto a clean work surface and make a well in the center. Dissolve the yeast in the lukewarm water. Pour the yeast mixture into the well, and gradually start incorporating them into the flour a little at a time. Stir in the pumpkin and the oil then add the salt. Knead the dough until soft, smooth, and elastic.

Let the dough rest, loosely covered with a plastic bowl, for about 10 minutes and then shape into long ropes.

Arrange the ropes, spaced apart, on a baking tray covered in parchment paper and let rise for 1 hour, loosely covered with lightly greased plastic.

Heat the oven to 350°F (175°C).

Bake the loaves until they sound hollow when tapped on the bottoms, 18 to 25 minutes, depending on the size. Let cool completely on a wire rack.

Difficulty

DESSERTS

CHAPTER SEVEN

SICILIAN CANNOLI

CANNOLI SICILIANI

Preparation time: 30 minutes + 1 to 1 1/2 hours resting time + 2 minutes cooking time

4 Servings

FOR THE PASTRY

3/4 cup plus 1 tbsp. (100 g) **all-purpose flour**

2 tbsp. (10 g) **unsweetened cocoa powder**

1 tbsp. plus 1/2 tsp. (15 g) **sugar**

2 tsp. (10 g) **unsalted butter, room temperature**

1 **large egg**

Salt

1 tbsp. (15 ml) **Marsala wine or rum**

FOR THE FILLING

8 3/4 oz. (250 g) **fresh ricotta, preferably made from sheep's milk**

1/2 cup (100 g) **sugar**

1 oz. (25 g) **candied fruit, roughly chopped**

1 oz. (25 g) **chocolate chips or semisweet chocolate roughly chopped**

1 oz. (25 g) **pistachios, roughly chopped**

Vegetable oil for deep frying

Confectioners' sugar for dusting

SPECIAL EQUIPMENT:

4 cannoli forms or stainless-steel dowels cut into 4-inch lengths

Difficulty

Method

For the pastry: Combine the flour, cocoa, sugar, butter, egg, and a pinch of salt in a bowl until combined; stir together with your fingertips until combined. Add the Marsala and stir together until a dough forms.

Turn out the dough out onto a clean work surface and knead until smooth and elastic. Form the dough into a disk and wrap tightly in plastic wrap, then let stand at room temperature for 30 minutes.

Meanwhile, prepare the filling. Using a rubber spatula, force the ricotta through a medium-mesh sieve into a bowl. Add the sugar, fruit, chocolate, and pistachios. Cover in plastic wrap and refrigerate until chilled, 30 to 60 minutes.

Using a pasta machine or a rolling pin, roll out the dough to 1/8 inch (2 mm) thick and cut it into 4-inch (10-cm) squares. Wrap the squares diagonally around a special cannoli form (or stainless-steel dowels cut into 4-inch lengths).

In a large deep skillet, heat 1 1/2 inches of oil over medium-high heat until shimmering. Place the cannoli forms with dough into the hot oil and fry until golden, 1 to 2 minutes. Remove from the oil, drain on paper towels, and let cool just enough to handle, then remove them from the cannoli forms.

Use a pastry bag to fill the cannoli with the ricotta filling, then dust with confectioners' sugar. Serve immediately (the moist filling soon makes the dough lose its crispness).

WHITE CHOCOLATE AND RASPBERRY TART
CROSTATA AL CIOCCOLATO BIANCO E LAMPONI

Preparation time: 1 hour 5 minutes + 2 hours resting time + 18 to 20 minutes cooking time

4 Servings

FOR THE CHOCOLATE SHORTBREAD CRUST
3/4 stick (95 g) **unsalted butter, room temperature, plus more for pan**
1/4 cup plus 2 tbsp. (85 g) **sugar**
Salt
2 **large egg yolks**
1/2 tsp. (3 ml) **vanilla extract**
1 1/4 cups (165 g) **all-purpose flour, plus more for dusting**
1/4 tsp. (1 g) **baking powder**
2 tbsp. plus 1 tsp. (9 g) **unsweetened cocoa powder**
Vegetable oil for plastic wrap

FOR THE FILLING
3 oz. (80 g) **raspberry jam**
7 oz. (200 g) **white chocolate, finely chopped**
1/4 cup plus 3 Tbsp. (100 ml) **heavy cream**
2 tsp. (10 ml) **light corn syrup**

FOR THE TOPPING:
9 oz. (250 g) **fresh raspberries**
Confectioners' sugar

Method

For the crust: With an electric mixer, beat together the butter and sugar, then stir in a pinch of salt, the egg yolks, and the vanilla. Sift together the flour, baking powder, and cocoa; add to the butter mixture, then knead briefly until you have a smooth dough. Form the dough into a disk. Wrap the disk in lightly oiled plastic wrap and refrigerate for 1 hour.

Heat the oven to 350°F (175°C).

Butter and flour an 8-inch (20 cm) tart pan with a removable bottom. On a clean, lightly floured work surface, roll out the dough to a 1/8-inch (3 mm) thick round. Fit into the tart pan, trimming the excess dough around the edges of the pan.

Spread the raspberry jam over the bottom of the tart shell, then bake until the shell is set, 18 to 20 minutes. Transfer the tart pan to a wire rack to cool. Remove the tart shell from the pan.

Place the chocolate in a heatproof bowl. Bring the cream and the corn syrup just to a boil in a saucepan, whisking to combine, then pour the mixture over the chocolate. Stir until you have a smooth, velvety cream. Let cool, then pour into the tart shell (it should reach the brim). Top with the outer edge of the tart with raspberries. Chill for at least 1 hour.

Dust the tart with confectioners' sugar just before serving. Serve with the remaining raspberries.

Difficulty

CHOCOLATE AND MINT PARFAITS

BICCHIERINI CIOCCOLATO E MENTA

Preparation time: 30 minutes + 2 hours cooling time

4 Servings

3 **sheets (7 g) gelatin, or 3/4 envelope
  granulated gelatin**
1 cup (250 ml) **milk**
1 cup (250 ml) **heavy cream**
3/4 cup (150 g) **sugar**
1 tsp. (5 ml) **peppermint extract**
Green food coloring
1 oz. (25 g) **dark chocolate, finely
  chopped**
**Fresh mint sprigs or unsweetened
  cocoa powder for garnish**

Method

Soak the gelatin sheets (if using) in water, then squeeze out any excess moisture.

In a medium saucepan, bring the milk and cream to a boil with the sugar. Reduce the heat to low; add the gelatin sheets (or granulated gelatin) and stir just until dissolved.

Divide this panna cotta mixture into 3 heatproof bowls. Leave the first as is. Flavor the second with the peppermint extract, then color it with a few drops of the green food coloring. To the final third, add the chocolate and stir until the chocolate is melted and the mixture is combined.

Strain a layer of the plain mixture into 4 dessert glasses and refrigerate until thickened.

Pour in a layer of the mint mixture and refrigerate to let it thicken (if it is too thick to pour, heat it gently to liquefy it). Finally add the chocolate mixture.

Refrigerate the parfaits at least 2 hours or until ready to serve. Garnish with fresh mint sprigs or a dusting of cocoa, if desired.

Difficulty

TIRAMISÙ

TIRAMISÙ

Preparation: 30 minutes + 2 hours chilling time

4 Servings

4 **large egg yolks**
10 tbsp. (125 g) **sugar**
1 1/3 cups (250 g) **mascarpone**
2 **large egg whites**
8 **savoiardi (crisp Italian ladyfingers)**
1 cup (200 ml) **cooled sweetened coffee**
5 tsp. (25 ml) **brandy (optional)**
Unsweetened cocoa powder for dusting

Method

Beat the eggs yolks with all but 1 tablespoon of the sugar in a metal bowl set over a saucepan of barely simmering water and using a whisk or hand-held electric mixer until the mixture has tripled in volume, 5 to 8 minutes. Remove the bowl from the heat. Beat in the mascarpone until just combined.

In a clean, dry bowl, using a clean, dry whisk or beaters, beat the egg whites together with the remaining 1 tablespoon sugar to stiff peaks. Gently fold the whites into the yolk mixture.

Dip the ladyfingers in the sweetened coffee (if you wish you can add a little brandy) and place them in the bottom of a dish (or in four small dishes or glasses). Then pour in a layer of the cream mixture and continue alternating layers of biscuits and cream. Refrigerate, covered, at least 2 hours or up to 2 days.

Dust with cocoa before serving.

Difficulty

CRÈME CARAMEL
CRÈME CARAMEL

Preparation time: 15 minutes + 50 minutes cooking time + 2 hours chilling time

4 Servings

FOR THE CARAMEL
1/4 cup (50 g) sugar

FOR THE CUSTARD
1 **lemon**
1 1/3 cups (330 ml) **whole milk**
1/4 cup plus 3 tbsp. (85 g) **sugar**
2 **large eggs**

Method

Heat the oven to 300°F (150°C).

For the caramel: In a saucepan over medium-high heat, combine the sugar and 1 tablespoon of water and bring to a boil.

Reduce the heat to medium and cook until the mixture is light brown and caramelized. Divide the caramel evenly between 4 ramekins or small dessert molds, swirling to coat the ramekins. Let cool.

For the custard: Using a paring knife, cut strips of zest from 1/2 of the lemon, avoiding the white pith. In a saucepan, combine the zest, milk, and sugar. Bring the mixture just to a simmer, stirring to dissolve the sugar, then remove from the heat. Remove and discard the zest.

In a bowl, beat the eggs. Whisking, add about a quarter of the milk mixture to the eggs. Then slowly add the remaining milk mixture, whisking as you go. Divide the custard among the ramekins or molds.

Prepare a hot water bath (bain-marie): Place the ramekins in a deep baking pan. Fill the pan with enough hot water to reach halfway up the sides of the ramekins. Bake in the middle of the oven until the custard is just set, 35 to 40 minutes.

Transfer the ramekins to a wire cooling rack, cool completely, and then refrigerate for at least 2 hours.

Before serving, invert each mold onto a dessert plate and serve the custards with caramel on top.

Difficulty

FROZEN ZABAGLIONE WITH MOSCATO D'ASTI PASSITO AND MELON PURÉE

ZABAIONE GELATO AL MOSCATO D'ASTI PASSITO SU FRULLATO DI MELONE

Preparation time: 15 minutes + 10 minutes cooking time + 2 hours freezing time

4 Servings

FOR THE ZABAGLIONE

6 **large egg yolks**
1 cup (200 g) **sugar**
3/4 cup (200 ml) **Moscato d'Asti or other Muscat wine**
8 1/3 cups (500 g) **whipped cream**

FOR THE MELON PURÉE

1 **medium cantaloupe, peeled, seeded, and cut into chunks**
1/4 cup (50g) **sugar**

Method

For the zabaglione: Whisk together the egg yolks and the sugar in a copper or metal bowl until frothy.

Fill a medium saucepan with 2 inches of water and bring to a simmer. Place the bowl over the simmering water. Whisking constantly, slowly add the Moscato. Continue whisking until the zabaglione thickens and reaches 175°F (80°C) on a candy or instant-read thermometer. Remove the bowl from the heat and let the zabaglione cool.

Gently fold in the whipped cream. Pour the mixture into a 6-inch-high by 7-inch-wide (15-18 cm) loaf pan and freeze until firm, at least 2 hours.

For the melon purée: Use a blender or food processor to purée the melon with the sugar.

To serve, remove the zabaglione from the loaf pan. Spoon a ladle of the purée into each dessert dish and arrange thin slices of the zabaglione on top.

Difficulty

SQUASH AND POPPYSEED HAND PIES

SFOGLIATINE DI ZUCCA E SEMI DI PAPAVERO

Preparation time: 40 minutes + 35 minutes cooking time

4 Servings

1/2 oz (20 g) **poppy seeds**
1 Tbsp. (20 g) **unsalted butter**
12 oz. (350 g) **butternut squash,
peeled, seeded, and cut into 1-inch
(3 cm) cubes**
5 tsp. (20 g) **sugar**
1 tsp. (10 g) **honey**
Salt
7 oz. (200 g) **frozen puff pastry, or
about 1 sheet, thawed**
Flour for dusting
1 **large egg, beaten**

Method

Coarsely grind the poppy seeds, using a coffee grinder or mortar and pestle, then place in a medium saucepan; add the butter. Heat over low until the butter is melted and the seeds are lightly toasted. Add the squash, sugar, honey, and a pinch of salt.

Continue cooking until the squash is cooked, but still thick. Let cool.

Heat the oven to 400°F (205°C). Line a baking sheet with parchment paper.

Roll out the puff pastry on a lightly floured surface to 1/8 inch (3 mm) thick. Using a 4-inch (10 cm) oval or round cookie cutter, cut out disks from the pastry.

Working with 1 disk at a time, brush the edge with a little beaten egg, then spoon some of the filling in the center. Fold the dough over the filling to form a half oval (or half circle), then crimp the edges with a fork to seal. Place on the prepared baking sheet. Repeat with the remaining ingredients.

Brush the tops with the beaten egg. Bake the pastries until golden, about 20 minutes.

Difficulty

GENOESE CHRISTMAS CAKE
PANETTONE GENOVESE

Preparation time: 30 minutes + 1 hour cooking time

4 Servings

1 1/3 cups (170 g) **all-purpose flour**
1 1/2 tsp. (5 g) **baking powder**
Salt
1/4 cup plus 1 3/4 tsp. (65 g) **unsalted butter, softened**
1/3 cup plus 3/4 tsp. (65 g) **sugar**
1 **large egg**
1/3 cup (50 g) **raisins, soaked in warm water for 15 minutes, then drained and squeezed of excess moisture**
1/4 cup (30 g) **hazelnuts, coarsely chopped**
3 tbsp. plus 2 tsp. (20 g) **pine nuts**
1 oz. (25 g) **total candied mixed fruit and candied cherries, diced**

Method

Heat the oven to 325°F (170°C). Line a baking sheet with parchment paper.

Sift together the flour, baking powder, and a pinch of salt in a bowl. With an electric mixer on medium-high speed, beat together the butter and sugar in another bowl until light and smooth. Beat in the egg, then stir in the flour mixture to combine. Gently fold in the raisins, hazelnuts, pine nuts, candied fruit, and candied cherries just to combine.

Form the batter into a ball, flatten it slightly, and place it on the prepared baking sheet. Bake for 50 to 60 minutes, or until golden brown.

Pine Nuts are Good for Love

There are about twenty species of pine that produce the pine nuts used in cooking (those nuts big enough to justify cultivating them as food). In Europe, there are two types of pine tree that produce large pine nuts: the common pine, Pinus pinea, and the Swiss stone pine, Pinus cembra. Extraordinarily rich in protein and antioxidants and high in energy, pine nuts have been consumed since prehistoric times. And since antiquity, they have been celebrated for their aphrodisiacal properties: the Latin poet Ovid, in his Ars Amatoria, considered them one of the few foods that could improve romantic capacity. In ancient Greece, pinecones, which conceal the pine nuts wrapped in a protective hull called a strobilus, symbolized the male sexual organ and induced fertility.

Difficulty

SHORTBREAD COOKIES
FROLLINI MONTATI

Preparation time: 15 minutes + 15 minutes resting time + 15 minutes cooking time

4 to 6 Servings

3/4 cup (165 g) **unsalted butter, softened**

1 cup plus 2 tbsp. (135 g) **confectioners' sugar**

2 **large eggs**

Finely grated zest of 1 lemon

1/2 tsp. (3 g) **vanilla extract**

1/2 tsp. (2 g) **salt**

2 3/4 cups (335 g) **all-purpose flour, sifted**

Method

Heat the oven to 350°F (175°C). Line a baking sheet with parchment paper.

Using an electric mixer fitted with the whisk attachment, beat together the butter and confectioners' sugar. Add the eggs, lemon zest, vanilla, and salt; mix until combined. Fold in the flour until just combined.

Use a pastry bag with a basketweave tip, pipe the dough in rounds onto the prepared baking sheets, spacing them at least 1 inch apart. Refrigerate for at least 15 minutes.

Bake the cookies for 13 to 15 minutes, or until golden brown. Let cool completely on a wire rack.

Whipped Short Pastry Dough

Whipped short pastry dough is a classic confectionary staple and is used to make shortbread cookies shaped with a pastry bag or cookie press, since the dough is much softer and creamier than that of the traditional recipe. These cookies are easy and quick to make, but are impressive for their flavor and tender crumb.

Difficulty

ITALIAN TRIFLE
ZUPPA INGLESE

Preparation time: 1 hour 30 minutes + 25 minutes cooking time

4 Servings

FOR THE CAKE LAYER

Unsalted butter for greasing

1 1/4 cups (180 g) **flour, sifted, plus more for the baking sheet**

8 (150 g) **large eggs, separated**

2 tbsp. (30 g) **sugar**

FOR THE OLD-FASHIONED PASTRY CREAM

1 cup (250 ml) **whole milk**

1/2 **vanilla bean, halved lengthwise, seeds scraped**

Zest of 1/2 lemon

7 **large egg yolks**

1/2 cup (100 g) **sugar**

1/4 cup (25 g) **flour, sifted**

FOR THE CHOCOLATE CUSTARD

2 cups (500 ml) **whole milk**

5 **large egg yolks**

3/4 cup (150 g) **sugar**

6 tbsp. (30 g) **unsweetened cocoa powder**

3 oz. (100 g) **dark chocolate, finely chopped**

FOR THE SYRUP

1/2 cup (100 ml) **water**

1/2 cup (100 g) **sugar**

1 **vanilla bean, halved lengthwise, seeds scraped**

1 2/3 cup (400 ml) **alkermes (Tuscan spiced liqueur) or Marsala wine**

Method

Make the cake layer: Heat the oven to 350°F (175°C). Grease 2 baking sheets with butter, then dust with flour.

In a bowl, beat together the egg yolks with half of the sugar. In a separate bowl, beat the egg whites with the remaining sugar. Fold in the yolk mixture and flour. Spread the batter into a 1/8-inch (3 mm) layer on the prepared baking sheet.

Bake for 10 minutes. Cool completely then cut into 3/4- by 2 3/4-inch (2 by 7 cm) rectangles.

Make the pastry cream: In a saucepan over medium heat, bring the milk just to a boil with the vanilla seeds, and the lemon zest. Remove from the heat.

Beat together the yolks and the sugar in a bowl. Add the flour; mix well. Whisk a quarter of the hot milk into the egg mixture, then whisk in the remaining milk. Return the mixture to the saucepan over medium heat and cook, whisking constantly, until the pastry cream simmers and thickens, about 1 minute. Remove from the heat, and whisk the cream until smooth. Transfer to a bowl and press plastic wrap directly onto the surface. Chill in the refrigerator.

Make the chocolate custard: Bring the milk just to a boil in a small saucepan. In a medium bowl, beat the yolks together with the sugar. Whisk a quarter of the milk into the eggs, then whisk in the remaining milk.

Return the mixture to the saucepan over medium heat and cook, whisking constantly until the custard simmers and thickens, about 1 minute. Remove from the heat. Add the cocoa and chocolate and whisk until the chocolate melts and the custard is smooth. Transfer to a bowl and press plastic wrap directly onto the surface. Chill in the refrigerator.

Make the syrup: Bring the water, sugar, and vanilla bean to a boil, stirring until the sugar dissolves. Remove from heat. Let cool completely, then stir in the liqueur.

Assemble and serve: Soak the cake in the syrup. Layer as follows: cake/pastry cream/ cake/chocolate custard/cake. Cut into squares. Garnish with the cherries and fresh fruit. Serve cold.

Difficulty

ALPHABETICAL INDEX OF RECIPES

INGREDIENTS INDEX

All photographs are by
ACADEMIA BARILLA

In the heart of Parma, one of the most distinguished capitals of Italian cuisine, is the Barilla Center. Set on the grounds of the former Barilla pasta factory, this modern architectural complex is the home of Academia Barilla. This was founded in 2004 to promote the art of Italian cuisine, protecting the regional gastronomic heritage and safeguarding it from imitations and counterfeits, while encouraging the great traditions of the Italian restaurant industry. Academia Barilla is also a center of great professionalism and talent that is exceptional in the world of cooking. It organizes cooking classes for culinary enthusiasts, it provides services for those involved in the restaurant industry, and it offers products of the highest quality. In 2007, Academia Barilla was awarded the "Premio Impresa-Cultura" for its campaigns promoting the culture and creativity of Italian gastronomy throughout the world. The center was designed to meet the training requirements of the world of food and it is equipped with all the multimedia facilities necessary for organizing major events. The remarkable gastronomic auditorium is surrounded by a restaurant, a laboratory for sensory analysis, and various teaching rooms equipped with the most modern technology. The Gastronomic Library contains over 11,000 books and a an impressive collection of historic menus as well as prints related to culinary subjects. The vast cultural heritage of the library can be consulted on the internet, which provides access to hundreds of digitized historic texts. This avant-garde approach and the presence of a team of internationally famous experts enables Academia Barilla to offer a wide range of courses, meeting the needs of both restaurant chefs and amateur food lovers. In addition, Academia Barilla arranges cultural events and activities aiming to develop the art of cooking, supervised by experts, chefs, and food critics, that are open to the public. It also organizes the "Academia Barilla Film Award" for short films devoted to Italy's culinary traditions.

www.academiabarilla.com

METRIC EQUIVALENTS

LIQUID/DRY MEASURES	
U.S.	**METRIC**
¼ teaspoon	1.25 milliliters
½ teaspoon	2.5 milliliters
1 teaspoon	5 milliliters
1 tablespoon (3 teaspoons)	15 milliliters
1 fluid ounce (2 tablespoons)	30 milliliters
¼ cup	60 milliliters
⅓ cup	80 milliliters
½ cup	120 milliliters
1 cup	240 milliliters
1 pint (2 cups)	480 milliliters
1 quart (4 cups; 32 ounces)	960 milliliters
1 gallon (4 quarts)	3.84 liters
1 ounce (by weight)	28 grams
1 pound	454 grams
2.2 pounds	1 kilogram

OVEN TEMPERATURES

°F	GAS MARK	°C
250	½	120
275	1	140
300	2	150
325	3	165
350	4	180
375	5	190
400	6	200
425	7	220
450	8	230
475	9	240
500	10	260
550	Broil	290